How to Grow Up Spiritually

How to Grow UP Spiritually

by **Steve Shamblin**

Shreveport • Lafayette
Louisiana

Huntington House, Inc.
1200 N. Market St., Shreveport, LA 71107

ISBN Number 0-910311-44-7

Typography and editing by Publications Technologies

Printed in the United States of America

Table of Contents

Acknowledgments

I want to give special thanks to my parents, Austin and Dorothy Shamblin, for their understanding of God's call on my life and their unwavering commitment to this call over the years. My gratitude also goes to Mr. A. G. Scarborough and his wife, Jean, who, along with my parents, have been such an encouragement and a help to me for so many years.

Special mention needs to be given to Pastor Ken Wright and his wife, Shirley, and Dr. Bruce Thompson and his wife, Barbara. Over the years, the influence of these two couples (who have been spiritual "moms and dads" to me) has been invaluable.

And an extra thanks to Carol Spicer at Publications Technologies for her fine editing work on this book.

Foreword

Spiritual maturity.

Has it evaded you?

Have you agonized before the Lord over what sort of spiritual giant He wants you to be?

Have you run into the same answers over and over?

Advice such as:

- Keep reading the Word?
- Have a daily quiet time?
- Praise the Lord continually?
- Keep your eyes on Jesus — not on men?
- Don't be anxious, but wait patiently on the Father?
- Evangelize everyone you meet?

Or maybe:

- Take your petitions constantly before the Lord, telling Him of your desire for spiritual maturity?

Or perhaps:

• Believe for a great personal maturity? In faith, take authority in this matter, believing that the Lord will honor His promises, your obedience and your faith – and will give you a great, supernatural maturity?

Are you confused?

Are you asking yourself just what avenue should you take to spiritual growth?

Well, consider this advice:

"Be patient until the Lord's coming. See how the farmer waits for the land to yield its valuable crop and how patient he is for the fall and spring rains. You too, be patient and stand firm.

"This is my prayer: that your love may abound more and more in knowledge and depth of insight, so that you may be able to discern what is best and may be pure and blameless until the day of Christ, filled with the fruit of righteousness that comes through Jesus Christ – to the glory and praise of God."

I'm sure that you recognize the work from which we have taken these gems of wisdom:

God's Word. This, too, is the source of author Steve Shamblin's instructions that follow in this superb book.

And here is his message that each reader must seek in its fullness:

You're a child of God!

And just as all children desire to become adults, so should we look forward to spiritual maturity.

Yet, just like the 16-year-old boy yearning to be treated like a man or the 13-year-old girl impatient to become a woman, we must not frustrate ourselves with that which will come to pass in its own good time.

Patience, patience!

Shamblin says we must be patient in our present state – open to the lessons that God daily is preparing for us.

Furthermore, we must be willing to serve where we are able to be of use – remaining eager in anticipation of the day in which we are better able to fulfill our potential.

But be careful:

Remember the humble lament of Albert Einstein:

"The more I learn, the more I realize that I do not know."

For should you ever decide that you have learned all that God has to teach you, rest assured that you have at least one more lesson in maturity ahead of you.

Babes in Christ

You're special.
You were put here for a reason.

So ...

The Lord has great hopes, desires and expectations for you – and for all of His children – just as any normal parent does.

However –

Unfortunately, our heavenly Father often has to lay aside many of these hopes and desires.

Why?

Because we haven't grown sufficiently and are not spiritually mature enough to embrace His great expectations.

Maturity.

Back in 1972, I attended a meeting where Youth With A Mission founder Loren Cunningham was telling of his vision for evangelism at the upcoming Olympics in Munich.

As I listened, I was moved in the depths of my spirit.

By the end of the service, I had become quite shaken — wonderfully so.

I felt compelled to become a part of this ministry.

But ... was it of me or of the Lord?

In my immaturity, I didn't know!

That afternoon, I attended a small meeting at a home where Mr. Cunningham was staying.

Again, that awesome feeling — a call? — came over me. I can only equate it to falling in love! My heart was going crazy.

I knew something was up.

But I couldn't put my finger on it.

Mr. Cunningham challenged each of us to help in the Munich outreach — as missionaries and evangelists.

I had never prayed about being a missionary — or anything else!

Sure, I had committed my life to

God in a very real way and had always figured my life was His to do with as He wanted.

Then, Mr. Cunningham asked which of us was willing to go to the Olympic games for Jesus.

Three of us volunteered.

Pleased, Mr. Cunningham handed us YWAM forms and noted: "I know the Lord's hand is in this, because I only have three applications left!"

My enthusiasm grew.

That evening, I came back to church to hear him speak again.

And by the middle of his sermon, I was really a mess.

What was going on inside of me? I asked the question of myself and the Lord. Was God actually trying to call me to the mission field?

Or was I just caught up in the moment, the excitement – the romance and idealism of obeying Mr. Cunningham's stirring appeal that we join him winning souls to the Kingdom?

I didn't know.

I was just a kid.

I had just gotten out of college and was working at a good job for the first time in my life. I was happy.

I had been dating the same girl for about three years. Everything was just fine.

Except ...

Except now God seemed to be calling me into ministry.

Why?

As I listened to Mr. Cunningham, I writhed in turmoil ... questioning, wondering. After the meeting, I spoke with Mr. Cunningham and went with him to the home where he was staying — where we talked into the early morning hours.

We talked and talked.

I basically asked every question in the world. Finally, he told me, "Steve, you need to just go home and ask God if you are to come, and let the Lord speak to you."

That seems simple enough now.

But at that time in my life, the idea of God speaking to His children was an absolutely new concept to me.

I remember thinking, "Loren, God may speak to *you,* but He hasn't told *me* much of anything.

Of course, that wasn't God's fault.

When I got home, I grabbed my Bible. Alone in the den, I just sat on the floor, put that wonderful book in front of me and waited on God.

I waited all night ...

By morning, all I could say that I heard was the verse in the eighth chapter of Deuteronomy where it talks about the hills rolling with milk and honey.

Well, that was really nice, but it was kind of hard to translate into any sort of answer about my call.

It was frustrating.

I just wasn't getting any more than this one verse of scripture.

Hours of prayer and meditation turned to days. The days went by without my hearing anything specific.

Yet ...

Yet, my heart was being swayed.

All my feelings and emotions were telling me "Go!"

But —

The Lord was waiting for me to come to the place of wanting His will, even if it meant staying home.

However, I didn't realize this was what was going on.

It was about the third or fourth

day I came to such a point of obedience. I came to the end of my "self."

I reached the point of "proper neutrality" which means that the bottom line now was God's will.

Yes, I still cared.

Yes, I still wanted to go.

But *my will* no longer was in control. I wanted to go where God wanted me to go.

I picked up the phone.

And I called a close friend, A.G. Scarborough, who had been a real help to me in my Christian walk. I told him, "It's been days now and all I can really say that I've received is this verse in Ezekiel 8, the first couple of verses."

He said, "Steve, I don't have time to read it or talk to you right now, so I'll call you back in a little while."

A short while later, in the middle of taking a shower, I realized I'd given A.G. the wrong verse.

I'd meant to say *Deuteronomy* 8!

I jumped out of the shower, called him back and said, "I've given you the wrong scripture!"

"Well," he laughed, "have you read Ezekiel 8?"

I flipped through my Bible.

And there, I saw the words:

"And it came to pass in the sixth year, in the sixth month on the fifth day of the month, as I sat in mine house, and the elders of Judah sat before me, that the hand of the Lord God fell upon me ..."

Then, A.G. asked me, "How long have you lived here in Raleigh, North Carolina?"

Because my father was in the military, my family had moved quite frequently when I was young.

But this time, I had stayed much longer than ever before.

Six years, as a matter of fact.

A.G. asked if I was sure. I was.

"What month is it today?" he asked – knowing the answer.

"June 5th," I replied. The fifth day of the sixth month. Just as in Ezekiel 8.

I saw the sign from God. He had sovereignly placed the verse in my mind in order to give me His call.

As we read the verse together again, A.G. quietly said, "I guess you're on your way, Steve."

Should we always expect such signs?

When we are babes in Christ, God

realizes our faith in Him has not really had time to grow a whole lot.

So, it's not unusual that, during these early stages, He will clearly speak in huge, obvious ways.

As babes in Christ, we need that.

I needed it.

I needed it because of what lay ahead.

When I left for the Munich outreach, I spent the next three months sleeping in a little tent in various spots around Europe.

Living conditions were rough.

I was confronted with many difficult situations. My natural tendency was to want to return home a number of times during that first year.

But each time that I would come to the place of wanting to give up and go home, the Lord would remind me of the events of His call on my life.

And I could not rationalize it away.

It had been too clear.

So, what does this mean to you?

The body of Christ is a family ... the family of God. And just like any group of relatives, we have members who are at different levels of maturity.

New Christians (or "converts")

usually realize they are now members of a denomination, but they often don't understand that they have been "born" into the family of *God*.

An unfortunate consequence of this is that the newest "child" doesn't always understand the importance of really getting to know our heavenly Father.

This often results in unnecessary struggles when trying to figure out God's will for us. It is important to remember that the more knowledge we have of God, the easier it is to know His will.

Growing up in the family of God.

Many of us, when we first come to Christ, never understand where we fit into His family. *Why?*

Because many of us never understood where we fit into our own earthly family, which can lead to insecurities and difficulties in growing up. It is normal when someone accepts Jesus as Saviour, that they are spiritually a babe in Christ, regardless of age.

What is *not* normal is for them to *stay* a babe in Christ!

Ephesians 4:14-15 says, "As a result, we should no longer be babes, swung back and forth and carried here and there with every wind of teaching that springs from human craftiness and ingenuity for devising error; but, telling the truth in love, we should grow up in every way toward Him who is the Head – Christ ..."

So let's analyze some of the character traits of a babe in Christ — hoping that we may recognize where we are and thus begin to grow up.

Instability and insecurity.

One of the more prominent characteristics of a new Christian is that of being swung back and forth. It is easy for babes to be swayed like this because they have yet to build a solid foundation.

They tend to go running around looking for spiritual milk.

Their greatest revelation and truth seems to come from whomever they last heard speak, but their great revelation usually lasts about as long as it takes them to go and hear another speaker.

And then,

And then, they think that's the greatest thing they've ever heard — once again.

Because of this tendency to be

swung to and fro, it can be both difficult and frustrating to get babes in Christ truly committed to anything, yet it is critical for them to get spiritual milk in order to have a proper foundation laid.

Frequently they're spiritual copycats.

Babes in Christ quite often lack their own spiritual identity and have a desire to emulate someone they believe is a "spiritual giant."

They often get ahead of their own maturity by attempting to prove their spiritual prowess by jumping all over the devil at any moment they feel is opportune.

Some years later, I was in a meeting when, as we were closing in prayer, the leader quietly pulled his hand out of mine, slipped down the hall – and fainted.

Several group members had just picked him up and put him on a bed in a back room when in rushed a new convert.

This well-meaning believer commenced to let the devil have it from every angle for many minutes. I stood by and witnessed all the commotion, yet did not sense the presence of the enemy.

I waited for the young convert to finish, and then turned to my friend on the bed and asked him if he knew what was wrong. (There's nothing unspiritual about asking a good question.)

My friend replied he had been so busy all day that he had not eaten.

That's all there was to it.

We *must* realize that babes in Christ have not yet learned a tremendous amount of spiritual sensitivity but as they grow up toward Him who is the Head, it will come.

So,

So here we have the babe in Christ trying to be a spiritual giant, but actually functioning out of spiritual insecurity.

As do most people who feel unsure, the babe adopts certain rules as a form of protection and cover-up.

To what effect?

Some of the first things we learn after salvation are that we need to pray, read the Bible, and witness. For the new Christian, these things can become instruments to secure God's love.

Quite innocently they begin to pray:

"Lord, I'll tell you what I'm going to do. I'm going to pray one hour every day; read the Bible two hours every day; witness three hours every day and go to 10 meetings every week."

Do the angels rejoice?

Is the Lord absolutely thrilled and astounded?

No, not really.

The Father knows He's dealing with a babe.

He knows that instead of one hour of prayer, He may get 15 minutes and that instead of two hours of reading the Bible, He may get 20 minutes.

What God will do, though, is take these small efforts and use them to lay a foundation upon which He can build. We can begin to see the problem the Lord (and leaders) have in dealing with babes. But in the midst of this, God *is* laying a foundation in them, for without that proper foundation, there can be no true and lasting spiritual growth.

Spiritual chicken pox.

Now there are a couple of very

common pitfalls down the road. Every child goes through earthly diseases of mumps, measles and chicken pox.

Thus it is, too, in the realm of the spirit.

There are two very common spiritual diseases that a babe in Christ must learn to overcome.

One is a spirit of competition.

We have been born out of a world which is literally programmed for competition.

It has been ingrained in us to get ahead of the other person – to compete for and win love and acceptance.

Now all of a sudden we are in a family where there *is* no competition. Living this new life in Christ is based on things like denial of self, giving instead of receiving, because the love of God is given through grace not by works.

Talk about a shock to the system!

No wonder it takes a while to absorb these new concepts and begin to live them.

Unfortunately, the new Christian sees his "mature" brothers and sisters competing for God's love.

A prime example of this are those pastors and leaders who are sadly insecure in the Lord and therefore cling to and control every area of their churches.

Fearful of letting go of their "power," they appear to the new Christian as competitors – instead of confident spiritual leaders who release authority as they grow secure in God.

Then, we must ask:

"Are we in this church modeling ourselves to be proper examples for babes in Christ?

"Or are we seen as contenders, fighting each other for God's love?"

There is no need to fight!

Here is one extremely important basic truth that I sincerely want each of you to grasp.

It is that *we are all equally loved by the Father!*

That's right!

There is no need for competition because once we have embraced God's love, we are free.

Yes –

Even free to grow up!

This brings us to yet another

question. Do you believe that God loves you as much as He loves His own Son, Jesus Christ? Let's look at John 17:23. "I in them and Thou in me, so that they may be completed into one, that the world may recognize that Thou has sent Me and has loved them as Thou hast loved me." With all of the mind's reason and logic, it may still be difficult to understand this one truth. But until we have it firmly in our hearts, not just our heads, we will continue to see young Christians strive to gain God's love through the work they do and the good deeds they perform.

Dear friends, it is the love of God that truly frees us up to grow.

Grab hold of that one thought!

Let me say that I don't understand how God can love me as much as He loves Jesus.

It doesn't make any sense to me either ... but He does!

And just because I don't *understand* doesn't keep me from *believing*.

The scriptures are full of this principle: believe – although at times you may not understand – just *believe!* Even as a little babe exercises a little bit of faith ... be childlike in your belief

... and act according to your believing.

Insecurity in God's love usually leads to another major problem for the babe in Christ to overcome –

The spirit of legalism.

Of course legalism is when we continue to try to *earn* God's love and favor.

This can creep into something as simple as our quiet time before the Lord.

Let me give you an example:

You wake up in the morning but it's a bit too late for your quiet time, so you promise God you'll spend time with Him later that evening, perhaps before bed.

Well, bedtime comes and you're just too tired for a quiet time.

But you're beginning to feel a bit guilty, so you promise God that in the morning you'll have *two* quiet times instead of just one! That seems to soothe the conscience and you're off to sleep.

It's typical for a babe to think "a quiet time a day will keep the enemy away." Not a bad philosophy, but the motive of the heart needs some work.

Our sole purpose for spending any

time with God is to give ourselves to him, to know Him, to fall more in love with Him ... not to try and gain something from Him.

Also, the babe in Christ is ...

Inexperienced in matters of righteousness ...

The babe in Christ is, of course, inexperienced in such things. In Hebrews 5:12-13, "... for whereas by this time you ought to be teachers, you stand again in need of someone to teach you the elementary principles of God's lessons; you have come to need milk and not solid food.

"Of course, anyone who feeds on milk is inexperienced in the matters of righteousness for he is an infant."

Here we are given the exhortation that by now we ought to be teachers.

The idea of "teacher" has to do with the example set forth in one's own life.

The question then becomes, how long have you known Jesus?

Six months?

One year?
Two years?
Three years or more?
Is the character of Jesus begin-

ning to show forth in your life?

Or, like a babe, are you still feeding on milk and therefore still inexperienced in the matters of righteousness?

Are you growing or stagnant?

Have you let the Lord deal with all areas of your life?

Or are you still keeping certain parts to yourself, refusing to let the Father change you?

As we walk toward spiritual maturity, we must be willing to allow God to mold us according to His image of us; as He sees us – perfect and complete – not as we see ourselves in the mirror!

In II Corinthians 5:21, Paul says, "God made Him who knew no sin to be made sin on our behalf, so that in Him we might share the righteousness of God."

What most of us tend to do is let God deal with some areas of our character but not with other areas.

For example: rock music

"Lord, I'll tell you what I'll do," we pray, "I'll let you deal with this area or that area of my character, but don't touch my rock music!"

Thus, by our refusal to let God deal with any area of our character, we stunt our spiritual growth.

Let's look at six concepts.

Now let's move on to the sixth chapter of Hebrews, verses1-3.

There we are going to take a quick look at six concepts that are referred to as the elementary teachings of Christ.

God expects us to learn these concepts in the *beginning* of our walk with Him ...

Not 20 years down the road!

I want to encourage you to spend more time getting to know what each area means.

Why? Because it's your foundation.

Repentance.

The first concept is repentance from dead works. Here the concept basically is that the Lord never takes pleasure in any of his children continuing to come to him over and over again asking forgiveness for the same thing.

When I was a young boy in church, I noticed that often the same people every Sunday would go forward at the altar call, asking for God's forgiveness.

I watched.

And I wondered why.

Why did the same ones always go up?

I believe that one reason is that they never learned what true repentance is.

They had fallen short.

They had failed to recognize dead works in their lives, too.

God wants us to understand these concepts so that we will not be fooling ourselves when it comes to repentance.

Faith.

The second concept mentioned is faith in God.

When we do not sufficiently learn about faith, we may wind up spending years doubting our own salvation.

Because of this, a new Christian may feel that God loves them ... when they're feeling good.

But –

When they're not feeling good, they may question their salvation.

In I John 1:7, we realize that the blood of Jesus cleanses us from *all* sin, not just *some* of our sins. In Ephesians 2:8-9, we come to the realization that we have been saved by grace ...

Not works!

To believe in these truths is to put your faith in God and to act accordingly.

The option is to continue to fluctuate in your own mind – in and out of salvation according to your mood swings – trying to insure your salvation by your own works.

Immersions.

Washings (or baptisms) is the third concept.

As we can see, the word is in plural form because the scriptures refer to more than one kind of baptism.

In Matthew 3, we see an example of water baptism, which symbolizes the washing away of our sins, the identification with death, and the resurrection of Jesus.

In John 17:20-23 and Galatians 3:27, we read of the baptism into Christ – that we may be completed into one, through the acceptance of Christ Jesus into our lives. And in Matthew 3:11 and Luke 11:13, we are told of the baptism of the Holy Spirit enabling us to walk in the power of His might and through His power to destroy the works of the enemy.

In Philippians 1:29 and Philippians 3:10, we see a baptism into the sufferings of Christ which comes our way as we walk after Him, not after this present world system.

Laying on hands.

The fourth concept is the laying on of hands.

Christians need to understand that we can't go running around laying hands on people indiscriminately.

Why?

Because by laying hands on someone, we are identifying with them in their situation.

We are looking to God to intervene and meet their needs.

Resurrection.

Resurrection from the dead is the fifth concept. It is important to be fully aware that Jesus has conquered death.

It holds no dominion over us, and when we die, we shall go to be with

Him. Thus, we are not to grow up fearing death.

Judgment.

The sixth and last concept mentioned is eternal punishment, or judgment.

This concept explains that through the blood of Jesus, our penalty has been paid in full.

We can face Judgment Day with hearts full of gratitude towards Jesus for bearing our punishment, and sparing us eternal anguish.

Build your house on a rock.

In order to lay a proper foundation for yourself, please study in depth these concepts which we have just briefly mentioned.

Although elementary, thcy will serve as a strong platform upon which to build your faith.

Paul tells us in I Corinthians 3:1-3 that babes in Christ tend to be very self-centered individuals.

They can display signs of jealousy and contentiousness.

They make unwise choices.

And they constantly desire attention.

It is this type of unspiritual behavior which can disrupt a group or church and eventually cause strife and division.

An example of this:

Look at I Corinthians 3:4-5 where we see the problem of improper identification.

Instead of exalting Jesus and His teachings, thereby protecting the unity of the body, these early Christians decided to exalt a mere man and his teachings, giving no thought at all to how this practice would destroy unity.

Today we see the same thing still going on within the body of Christ.

Instead of "I hold with Paul or Apollos," it is, "I hold with Oral Roberts, or Jimmy Swaggart, or Kenneth Copeland," again exalting the teachings of mere men over the teachings of Christ.

Paul is very clear as to what he calls this kind of action:

Unspiritual!

It is behaving as though you were never saved.

We often see this evidenced within Christian organizations as well as in our churches. There is often great division between different departments caused by a selfish attitude towards one's own department or project, and not really caring about any others within the church or organization.

This invites a spirit of competition.

Instead of functioning as a family, the Christian organization begins to function as a religious institution with everyone looking out for their own good.

Looking back at these different traits which reflect immaturity, it is easy to see how important it is for us to grow up.

But first –

In order to grow up, we must be willing to give up.

In I Peter 2:1, the Lord provides us with a very specific list of areas which we must be willing to deal with ... or the babe in Christ will never grow up spiritually.

"Therefore lay aside all malice and all deceit, all pretense, envy, and slander ..." we are told.

Malice – dealing with hatred and bitterness – is the first one mentioned.

Malice.

God asks us to give up *all* of our bitterness, *all* of our resentment, and *all* of our hatred of other people.

And when God says *all*, He means *all*.

Therefore we must see that it is totally possible for us to fully release and forgive people, or God would not have demanded it of us.

So then the important questions become:

• "Is there any malice in your heart?"

and

• "Are you presently holding any bitterness, resentment, or hatred against another?"

Be careful about malice's poison!

In ministering around the world, I have seen many who have struggled for years refusing to forgive boyfriends and girlfriends who have hurt them in relationships.

I've seen many more who have struggled in forgiving a parent who abused them, molested them sexually, and countless other difficult situations.

But again, the question is:

"Are you willing to let it go and

humble yourself, ask God's forgiveness for the bitterness in your heart, and then forgive the one who hurt you?"

Deceit

Deceit is the next area mentioned, with manipulation and lying as its common associates.

Holding onto these areas prevents God from being able to use us to His full intent. We simply cannot fool or manipulate Jesus! And until we are ready to properly deal with these traits before the Lord, they will continue to cause us to be robbed of growing up into the image of Christ and all He has in store for us.

They will block our path to maturity.

For example: I was speaking recently in Sweden, and challenged the people to deal with these very areas.

A young man stood up in the back of the class and nervously shared that he was afraid to be known for who he was because he feared that if people found out who he really was *inside,* they would reject him. At that instant I felt the Lord quicken me to ask how many others were in the same position as this young man.

Almost everyone stood, confessing they felt the same.

So all of a sudden, everyone came to realize that we were all fearing the same thing: *that if you know me for who I am, you're going to reject me.*

And of course the only way to be free is to be known for who you are which, therefore, means you must be willing to deal with deceitfulness.

Pretense is next. Before we came to the Lord, we all wore masks, and out of fear pretended to be other than what we were.

Pretense.

God promises not to despise a broken and contrite heart, so even though we have falsely covered up for so long, it is time to let our hearts be open and to show ourselves for who we are in the security of God's love. The church needs to come to this point before healing can take place.

Jesus lived a transparent life before God and man, and He expects nothing less from us as we live out our life before Him.

Envy.

The fourth area with which we must deal is envy. Because we are all equally loved of the Father, we must come to realize that our source of security is from God's love, thereby freeing our lives from insecurity, jealousy, and envy.

Envy comes from selfishness.

It is the immature and often selfish desire for love and attention that produces envy, and revolves around the thought that someone else is receiving what you feel *you* should be getting. What you are actually doing is attempting to substitute God's love and attention for outside sources of gratification.

Slander – an outcropping of envy – is the fifth area with which we will deal.

Slander.

Brought about by our own insecurity in God's love, we often find ourselves criticizing and slandering others in order to reduce them to a level we find acceptable. Then, unwittingly, we discover that criticism and slander have become an integral part of our character.

Keep in mind that any time you hear someone criticize another, it is because they are insecure with God's love and striving for attention through slander and criticism.

And this is where the challenge comes in ... at this point I would like to encourage you to get alone with God and go over each of these five areas and begin to pray for God's conviction.

Realize this:

You have nothing to fear in God's conviction because this is how He lets us know we are loved and that he cares enough to let us know when we are doing wrong. So don't be afraid of the conviction of the Lord, even though it may hurt, because it is the truth that will set you free. In light of this, spend time with God going over and praying through each of these areas. Then, as it says in I Peter, we will realize a complete freedom.

But don't expect a quick fix.

Yes, we will find true release from each one of these areas – why? – because we have been willing to allow the Lord to speak truth into our lives and have been willing to act upon the truth that we may be set free.

However, this is something that you cannot do in just a few minutes.

No, you need time alone with God.

God is not only supernatural, He is also very practical, and throughout this text we will be talking about practical Christianity.

What does the Lord require?

God is not asking us, as babes, to go out and take on the world, but He is asking us to do exactly what we are capable of doing.

Unfortunately, most Christians don't believe that God means what He says.

Therefore, after years of salvation they still have not laid aside all malice, deceit, pretense, envy, and slander.

And what is the result?

They are still walking in spiritual immaturity.

God is a wise Father Who will not be mocked.

He will not release authority and responsibility to those in His family who have never grown up.

He is always faithful and just, desiring to see us become stronger and more dependable.

Yet, He handles us with a balance of love, patience, grace, and discipline. Therefore, in our dealings with babes, we must follow the example God shows us: times of grace, and times of discipline which must be clothed in His love.

The most important concepts a babe can learn are about his heavenly Father and the wonderful provisions which are his through Christ.

Faith is simple.

Basically, our Lord is asking babes to simply get to know Him, their new Father, and His love for them through Jesus.

It is the embracing of God's love that frees us to grow up.

Contrary to this, we find others trying to feed these young Christians all manner of information, such as Charles Finney's systematic theology, or their church's own denominational theologies.

These may be just fine, but not appropriate for babes to digest.

Isaiah 28:9-10 says it very well:

"Whom will He teach knowledge, and who shall be made to understand the message?

"Babes just weaned from the milk, just drawn from the breasts?

"For it is precept upon precept, precept upon precept, line upon line, line upon line, here a little, there a little."

Children of God

"If, however, we walk in the light, as He Himself is in the light," notes I John 1:7, "then we enjoy fellowship with one another, and the blood of His Son Jesus cleanses us from all sin."

Note this warning:

"No one who remains in Him practices sin," I John 3:6-8 adds. "Whoever practices sinning has neither seen Him nor known Him. Dear children, no one should deceive you. He who practices righteousness is righteous, just as He Himself is righteous. He who practices sin belongs to the devil, for from the beginning the devil has sinned. For this purpose the Son of God appeared, to destroy the works of the devil."

One simple truth that is vital to our growth is this: knowing we are cleansed from all our sin because we have truly repented.

Too many of God's children believe they are cleansed from some of their sin, but not all of their sin. One reason for this confusion is the glorification of sin. People often become obsessed with the magnitude of their sin to the degree that they exalt it over God's power to cleanse them.

The consequential philosophy then becomes, "We cannot help ourselves but sin."

But that's a lie.

It may come as a shock to some, but after accepting Jesus, we do not have to continue to sin any more! Look at I John 2:1 – where we are told, "Dear children, I write you these things so you may not sin, and if anyone does sin, we have a counsel for our defense in the Father's presence, Jesus Christ the Righteous One." After reading these verses we can come to a very basic conclusion: if we are continuing to sin it is because we love the sin more than we love God and His Holiness.

Therefore, one of the first principles that we are to learn and understand as new Christians is that our sins have been forgiven, and that God is trying in every way to see that we grow up knowing freedom and victory over sin.

God loves us.

God asks us not to sin because He loves us – and we choose not to sin because we love Him.

Another character trait of a child in God's family is the concept of coming to know the Father as it reads in I John 2:13: "I have written you, children, because you have come to know the Father." This concept of *coming to know* involves learning how to recognize our Lord and relate to Him.

It is learning to relate to and recognize the Father that encourages that love/trust relationship with Him.

It is also through learning to recognize and relate that one's spiritual sensitivity begins to develop.

As we come to Him, an *incredible thing* happens.

He begins to re-parent us; an extremely important process that allows God to work through all the hurts, wounds, and damages of our lives no matter how young or old we are.

If we cooperate with God and allow Him to operate within us during this time of re-parenting, our love and trust for him will just grow and grow.

Wondering why.

Unfortunately, many people won't allow God to re-parent them. Thus they can never be secure in his love and they will spend years wondering why.

Yes, it can hurt to be re-parented, but it is a good hurt, a hurt that leads to healing and wholeness.

Childhood is to be a good time of growing up.

It is a time when one's relationship with God begins to solidify into a precious love/trust relationship which can never be broken.

It is the time when God begins to equip us spiritually for that which lies ahead.

In John 2:20 we see another way that God wants to equip us: "Besides, you have an anointing from the Holy One and you know all things." In I John 2:27 we are again told: "As for you, the anointing you have received from Him remains within you, and you stand in no need of teaching from anyone; but as His anointing instructs you about everything and is true and is no lie, so keep in union with Him just as it was taught you." Did you realize that as a child in God's family you have been given an anointing? The word anointing here translates to the "endowment of the Holy Spirit."

Many young Christians cry out to God to be anointed, failing to embrace that which they have already been given.

So another basic question here is: What kind of relationship do you have with the Holy Spirit? We must understand that Jesus has given the Holy Spirit as our anointing to equip us for that which lies ahead as we grow in Christ.

A spurned present.

But just because it is given, not all accept it.

It is like salvation – Jesus has freely given salvation to all men, but not all accept His gift.

My encouragement to you then as a child is get to know your anointing – the Holy Spirit – from whom all other gifts shall flow.

"And now, dear children, remain in Him so that when He appears we may have confidence and may not shrink in shame from Him at His coming." (I John 2:28) We'll face many tests and challenges as we grow in faith.

It is for this reason that we find it imperative to learn how to "remain in Him," to abide and rest in His presence.

We needn't run away —

We needn't be anxious, nervous or uncomfortable in the presence of God.

As we begin to trust the Father we can be more confident that no matter what the obstacle, we will overcome through the victory of Jesus Christ. I have been in churches all over the world and would have to say that the spiritual maturity of most church groups is that of a child — because they have never learned to rest or abide in His presence.

Relax in His presence.

The reason most Christians never mature spiritually is because they never learn to abide and rest in the love and presence of God the Father.

As a result, instead of overcoming the tests, trials and challenges that lie ahead as they grow up, they are overwhelmed by them.

Dear children, learn what it is to

rest and abide in his presence.

It is truly exciting to realize that as children our heavenly Father wants us to understand the meaning of love.

In I John 3:16, He tells us, "We understand the meaning of love from this, that He laid down His life on our behalf, and we ought to lay down our lives on behalf of the brothers."

No greater love.

Most people search all their lives and never come to a true understanding of what love is.

In this one simple verse of scripture, we see that a choice was made by Jesus to lay down His life – for you, for me, as undeserving as we are.

This is what love is ... a choice made from the heart.

A choice, not a feeling.

Unfortunately, the world would have us believe that love is just emotion – thereby enabling us to deny responsibility for how our lives are ruled and influenced.

But God does not want His children to grow up being controlled by feelings, but rather by the Spirit of God incorporating true love.

When we fully understand the

meaning of love, new feelings can be created within us by simply walking in that love.

We begin to act unselfishly, choosing our highest standards for God, others and ourselves.

Why? Because love is not selfish.

Jesus laid down His life as a great unselfish act of love – for us and God.

His love is truly amazing and has set the best example we could follow!

In verse 18 of I John 3, we read, "Dear children, let us not love in word and tongue, but in deed and truth." We have just learned the true meaning of love, and now we see God showing us how to properly function in that love.

He tells us not to love in word and tongue, which refers to a bunch of hot air! Many Christians are "serving" God in this way.

Hot air Christians.

They talk a lot, but their hearts are far from Him.

Understanding what love is, God tells us to love in deed and truth, referring to how we must embrace truth and put it into action by making a conscious decision to do so.

By not acting out our faith, by using just empty words, the consequences can be severe, but by serving him in deed and truth, our rewards are as presented in verse 19: "In this way we shall become aware that we belong to the truth, and in His presence we shall set our hearts at rest." The blessing of serving God in this way is that we will become aware that we belong to the truth, something which many Christians miss.

Can you imagine a child not knowing he belongs to his family? Let's say it's supper time and your mom calls you in from playing outside.

A slap in the face.

You come into the house and stand there looking around, staring at your parents and then you make an incredible statement: "I don't feel like I belong here." Your parents are shocked and say, "What do you mean you don't feel like you belong here?" You respond, "I just don't feel like I belong here and I think I'll go visit some other houses and see if I belong there." As strange as it may seem, this is what many Christians do to God.

They come into His presence, look around, and then make the same ridiculous statement, "I don't feel like I belong here." This is why God is teaching us about love and how to love properly.

If we will love God in deed and truth, we come into a blessed understanding that we do belong to the truth and our hearts will come into that place of rest in Him.

Many Christians try to turn this principle around, in that they want God to somehow show them that He loves them, and if and when He does, then they will serve Him.

Don't expect results.

This turned-around method will never work because God has already shown and proven His love for us by laying down His Son on our behalf.

It is our responsibility to embrace this truth and act upon it, thereby beginning to produce what we have wanted all along ... the knowledge and feeling that we belong to the truth.

In light of all this, let me ask you to seriously consider and re-examine how it is you are loving God.

"And this is His command, that we put our faith in the name of His Son Jesus Christ and that we love one another as He commanded us. He who obeys His commands remains in Him and He in him. By this we know that He remains in us, through the Spirit whom He has given us." We are commanded to put our faith in Jesus, but many Christians want to look at this as an option in their walk with the Lord.

But it is certainly not an option; it is a command!

I would like you to examine the establishment of this principle in two very important areas of your life: intercession and spiritual warfare.

Spiritual warfare and intercession, although potentially new concepts to a child, were never meant to be overwhelming.

God would not have us frightened.

Nor would He allow us to get involved before we are prepared.

Like learning to swim, the first thing we must do is get our feet wet! I remember my first experiences with intercession and spiritual warfare ... definitely an intimidating time. I was under the impression that I was only to pray God's thoughts.

But I wasn't overly confident that I was even hearing God's thoughts.

But one of the things I learned was, when beginning in this area of our walk, there is a freedom in God to fail and still be loved which should encourage us not to remain silent for fear of making a mistake.

Just like a parent with a child who is learning how to talk, He doesn't care so much what we say as long as we make a prayerful attempt to speak.

Remember when you learned to ride a bike for the first time? You got up, you fell, you got up again and continued on in this way until you learned to ride well.

Try, try again.

We need to have this same kind of attitude towards intercession and spiritual warfare, realizing they are extremely important aspects of maturity.

But there must be a time of learning – in which we are free to fail and still be loved and accepted.

What a blessing it is to know that our Father realizes and understands that we are children! I can remember once being invited to a friend's house for supper.

The time came for the children to go to bed.

All seemed to go smoothly and about an hour went by with complete silence.

Then suddenly, here they came down the hallway, having spent the last 60 minutes dressing up in mom's and dad's clothes, perfume filling the air, lipstick fairly close to the lips, hats falling down over their wide-awake eyes, stumbling as they tried to walk in shoes too big! Is this how God often sees us? Do we come into His presence to do battle with the enemy as children unprepared and too immature to put on the armor of God?

Getting ready.

Here we come as babes to put on His armor, with the helmet of salvation falling down over our eyes preventing us from seeing where we're headed; the breastplate of righteousness falling down to our waist; girding our loins with the belt of truth, just to have our pants fall down; then using one hand to hold them up!

So, we strain and —

With our free hand we ponder which we should grasp, the sword or the shield, deciding on the sword and asking God to take the shield and guard the rear! Then, as we reach down for the sword, we discover it's a lot heavier than we imagined.

After much straining, we finally manage to get the sword off the ground.

And suddenly off we go, wherever the sword leads us, we follow ...

Just trying to hang on.

Shod in our shoes of peace –

– which are many sizes too big for us ...

... we go clomping all over heaven!

The Father quickly sees what's happening, comes running in and gets all the angels out of our way.

So after about 55 minutes of romping in this condition, we fall down exhausted but pleased, knowing that if we're this tired, the devil is hurting!

Hallelujah for a patient God!

As we lay there worn out and thinking, the Lord comes over to us and heals any self-inficted wounds (which we thought were cheap shots from the enemy).

Then He softly reassures us:

"My child, you have not yet learned what it is to rest and remain in my presence."

Unfortunately, we probably didn't hear that at all!

So our Heavenly Father picks us up, re-dresses us in properly sized clothes suitable for our level of spiritual maturity, and encourages us with His love.

Immaturity.

When I was about 22 years old, a friend and I attended a Christian seminar where word circulated that there was going to be a deliverance session.

Naturally, we wanted to watch and learn what we could. So, we stayed and took it all in.

I was impressed to say the least.

But being a babe in Christ, I really didn't have the foggiest idea of what was going on.

So my friend and I went back to our room.

A short while later there came a knock at the door.

As we opened it, a young man stood before us and proclaimed, "I've got all these demons in me and I want you to cast them out!"

Who, me?

Before I could even utter, "You've got to be kidding!" my friend invited him in. Instead of confessing to this poor soul that I had no idea what I was doing, I gave in to the world's way of covering up, and pretended I had it all together.

I faked it.

Now remember that my friend and I were just babes.

What we sorely lacked in spiritual authority, we made up for in physical authority.

We were both in excellent physical condition, so we simply used what we had and began to lay hands on this fellow. Well, it certainly didn't take us long before we had him flat on the ground, both of us on top of him, pushing him right through the floor with all our might!

Apparently our only strategy was to "mash" those demons right out of him. The next thing we knew, he jumped up clutching his throat, gasping, "I can't breathe! I can't breathe!"

To our astonishment, he struggled toward the door and made an *amazing* statement –

"I think I'll go elsewhere to have the rest of these demons taken care of," he gasped over his shoulder.

Today, I know that the real truth:

He probably didn't have any demons in the first place.

But I was too immature to know how to handle the situation. We almost killed the poor guy with our righteous and well-meaning enthusiasm before he retreated. And the whole experience unfortunately taught me "fear of the devil" instead of "faith in Jesus."

That is where a lot of Christians are today – secretly trying to deal with a fear of the devil.

We are not to fear.

That is why God, as our heavenly Father, wants us to learn what it is to put our faith in the name of His Son Jesus –

So we will not grow up in the family of God fearing the devil.

We are to be confident in the Lord.

As children, we must establish where our confidence and security lie.

In addition to our faith in Jesus, the scriptures mention three other areas.

As we see in I John 5:13, one of those areas is in knowing in whom we believe, walking in fellowship with Him, not fear ... "I am writing this to you who believe in the name of God's Son in order that you may know that you have eternal life."

The second area is in finding confidence in knowing our inheritance and authority in Christ when we read in I John 4:4, "You are from God, dear children, and have defeated them, because the One in you is greater than the one in the world."

And I John 3:8 tells us, "For this purpose the Son of God appeared, to destroy the works of the devil."

As we begin to grow in faith and confidence in who our heavenly Father is, we begin to exercise our authority and destroy the works of the enemy.

Growing pains.

The principle of putting our faith in Jesus is critical to our spiritual growth.

The problem is that we don't like to exercise our faith any more than we like to exercise our seldom-used muscles.

It hurts!

But we must persevere ... we must continue to exercise our faith if we are to get stronger! So let me encourage you to learn about intercession and spiritual warfare for they are indispensable tools in overcoming the challenges that lie ahead as we grow up in Jesus.

Young Men and Women of God

As we begin to practice the principles outlined in Chapters One and Two, we find evidence of the fruits of the Spirit coming into our lives.

Vigorous young men

In I John 2:13-14, we read, "I am writing you, young men, because you have conquered the evil one," and "I have written you, young men, because you are vigorous; God's message stays in your hearts and you have conquered the evil one." We see here that young men are "vigorous." This translates as "forceful, mighty, and powerful," all referring to spiritual attributes.

It is interesting to note that the reason young men are referred to as vigorous is because of the next statement in that verse which tells us,

"God's message stays in your hearts." I'm sure it's a blessing to God to see us come into the place where His message stays in our hearts.

No longer are we walking with Him one day but not the next; no longer are we riding the roller-coaster of emotions, committed and trusting God one day but not the next.

Fruit in our lives.

Finally, the mark of impending maturity becomes reality, and the message of God stays in our hearts, firmly rooted, and enabling us to be forceful, mighty and powerful in His Name.

Because we have become consistent in our commitment to God, He can now produce consistent fruit in our lives.

One of the first fruits we will see is the concept of young men "having conquered the evil one." As children in Christ, we have learned to put our faith in Jesus.

Because we have learned faith and not fear, we are to have no fear of demons or the devil. But it is typical of the devil to try and instill this fear in us while we are yet babes.

The fact is, anyone can scare a little baby or child.

That is why when most Christians begin to grow up, there may be an embarrassing fear which they are not only ashamed to admit to, but are not sure why it's there or how to get rid of it.

We simply need to recognize what has taken place; that the enemy has tried to instill fear in our hearts, through any number of ways, and we must confess that fear, as well as any fear of the devil or demons, renounce it as the lie it is, and ask the Lord's forgiveness for believing that lie.

Then we can begin to walk in the security and confidence of our Saviour.

Conquerors

With this in mind, let's look at the concept that says young men have conquered the evil one.

In order to conquer the enemy, three practical things must take place.

First, a young man must learn to discern the works of the enemy which, of course, come from the actual and practical development of spiritual sensitivity.

No longer are we being completely taken advantage of and fooled.

We are now learning to identify the enemy's handiwork.

The second principle the young man must have is an understanding of the battle.

How to fight back

We must know what the enemy is attacking and how he is accomplishing the attack; which, in turn, leads us to the third principle of exercising our faith in Jesus in order to destroy the works of the enemy.

Because these concepts and principles are so closely interwoven, it becomes clear why it is so important to put our faith in the Name of Jesus while we are still children, for without exercising our faith, there won't be a whole lot of victory in our battles.

As we go further into the concepts of what it is to be a young man of God, we want to look at the relationship between Paul, a mature man of God, and Timothy, his disciple still young in the Lord.

Let's pick up the relationship in I Timothy 4:12, "Let no one think little of you because of your youth; instead, become in speech, in behavior, in love, in faith, in purity, an example before those who believe." I would like to examine the first portion of that verse referring to not letting anyone think little of you because of your youth.

Paul is presenting Timothy and us with a very important principle, that as we continue to grow up and respond to God's call, we are going to have to guard against the fear of man.

This warning tells Timothy not to let the expectations of man limit him in the call of God.

Let's look at the practicality of this.

As the Lord has allowed me to travel and minister over much of this world, I have seen the same situations over and over again.

When a young person receives a call to go to the mission field, that call is always accompanied by feelings of excitement and great joy.

Generally the first people he wants to share the good news with are his parents, but unfortunately, he is often met with a less than enthusiastic attitude. Parents have a way of asking what seems to be more than their share of questions; not that these questions are wrong, but the parents must realize that the inability of the young person to answer all their questions up front does not have any reflection on whether or not God did call their son or daughter.

For example, I remember when the Lord put His call on my life. I believed I was to join an organization called Youth With A Mission –

But that was all I knew.

When I went to share this with my parents (I was 21 years old at the time), they had some very good questions, such as, "What is Youth With A Mission?"

I answered, "Well, I don't know very much about them."

Then they asked, "What are you going to be doing with them?"

I answered, "Well, I don't know."

They continued with, "How long are you going to be gone?"

I answered, "Well, I don't know."

Again they asked, "How are you going to exist financially?"

I answered, "Well, I don't know."

Sometimes, dear friends, we must realize that God does not always give us all the answers along with His call, but we must also realize that if He has seen fit to place that call on your life, He certainly expects you to respond! Another great obstacle young people run into when they accept the call of God in their lives is the pressure of society and parents for them to go to college.

Too often the reality of the call is overlooked in light of the parents' natural desire for their child to attend college. What occurs is that parents require their child to at least try to get a degree before they will give their blessing – spiritual or financial.

There is an interesting verse in Matthew 10:36-38, "He who loves father or mother more than Me is not worthy of Me, and he who loves son or daughter more than Me is not worthy of Me. And he who does not take his cross and follow after Me is not worthy of Me."

It is sad but true, that when God puts His call on a life, the sources of greatest resistance are often parents, family, pastor, other church leaders and even Christian friends. With this kind of "help" the enemy doesn't have to do much to discourage you.

After speaking to their parents, young people often turn to their pastors in hopes of finding a more understanding response.

Sadly, in the vast majority of cases, if a young person is called to go to the mission field outside of their own denomination, they are virtually on their own.

How must God feel when He sees a local church give thousands of dollars to support people they don't even know, and yet ignore young people whom God has called from within their fellowship.

It is my prayer that the Lord will continue to bless those pastors and churches whose vision for His work is not so restrictive and introspective.

We must recognize the importance of what Paul told Timothy about guarding against the "fear of man."

In the second part of I Timothy 4:12, Paul is encouraging Timothy to become an example before those who believe. This is a tremendous responsibility given to us as young men of God. We are encouraged to set an example in our speech, our behavior, and our actions displaying love, faith and purity.

So I ask, how are you doing in becoming an example in each of these areas? I encourage you to take some time to examine yourself before the Lord in each of these character traits.

How am I doing in my speech in becoming an example before those who believe? Be completely open and honest before the Lord, giving Him time to both convict you where it is needed and to minister to you.

Then go on to the next trait until they have all been covered and touched by the Lord. This is practical Christianity, friends, and the Lord will begin to release responsibility to us as we mature in these things.

In I Timothy 4:13, we read, "Till I arrive, devote yourself to the public reading, the preaching and the teaching." Paul is teaching Timothy a simple but very important principle here, and that is to "learn to continue in the way God is leading you." It is obvious from this verse that God's leading in Timothy's life involved public reading, preaching, and teaching.

Paul was exhorting Timothy to recognize what God had already spoken into his life and to pursue that.

The warning here is not to become so preoccupied with vision and the future that you forget to continue on in the things that have already been laid before you.

This common problem is often responsible for much anguish and confusion because it is so easy for the young person in God to become preoccupied with the future. We would all like a vision for our entire life, yet we often forget what the Lord has already spoken to us. In our immaturity, we are unable to remain faithful in the little things while searching for that elusive big picture.

Again let me share a little bit out of my own life:

The Lord called me to the mission field in 1972, and all I knew of my future was that I was headed for the Olympics in Germany and that I was going to a Youth With A Mission school of evangelism following that.

Then as I prayed, the Lord would again share with me what I was to do for Him during the next three months. This went on for my first three years as a missionary and it was not always looked upon as a sign of my spiritual maturity.

There were times when I was asked by my parents, friends or pastor about what I was going to be doing. The only thing I could share with them was what the Lord shared with me ... which never seemed to amount to more than the next three months! I felt so frustrated when I was often asked, "What is the vision the Lord has given you?" and had to reply that I just didn't have one yet.

But that didn't mean I wasn't being faithful and staying before the Lord for His vision.

In retrospect, I realize that the call and plan of God for my life has been a progression; as I walked in obedience to His commands, He revealed more and more to me, and still continues in this way.

To me, entering into the depths of God's call and vision for one's life is a walk of obedience and learning to "continue in the way" as Paul instructed Timothy.

However,

Paul also tells Timothy in verse 14, "Do not neglect the gift in you that was given to you through a prophetic utterance with the laying on of hands by the elders." Our reaction may be, What is that gift? How can I identify it and not neglect it? We may even feel that the Lord hasn't given us any special gift at all.

Of course that isn't true because we have all been given Jesus and the Holy Spirit which are the two most precious gifts you will ever receive.

As a matter of fact, all other spiritual manifestations will flow out of your relationship with our Lord Jesus and the Holy Spirit.

Don't neglect your gifts.

As we have acknowledged these gifts, we now must determine what it is we are going to do with them.

But first we must ask, have we been neglecting them? The interesting concept of "don't neglect" refers to a stirring up of the gifts within you, and how do we do that? Certainly not by avoiding people, problems, confrontation situations, and circumstances which make you uncomfortable.

Don't miss chances for growth.

When we avoid these times, we relinquish unique opportunities for growth, and as a result, often tend to look at ourselves and feel we don't have any gifts simply because all we have done is hide in a corner and blame God for not blessing us.

Let me share an example:

I was once a member of a ministry team in Japan.

One Sunday, the leadership asked me and another member of the team, Kathy, if we would go to a local church and speak at the Sunday services.

Now that didn't sound at all threatening until they began to share some "particulars" about this church.

First of all, it was in the "red light" district of Osaka.

Then, we were told that the congregation would consist of some Christians, some drunks, some drug addicts, and various other types of citizenry.

Then we were told that this church had to use bodyguards to help protect the speakers!

The assignment took on a new light.

Now I was never one to shy away from a challenge and neither was Kathy, but both of us began coming up with "valid" reasons why it would probably be much better if someone else went instead of us.

The leadership, being what it was, persisted and off we went.

When we arrived, it was total chaos.

All I can say is that our first impression of that church was that it was like a circus! People were walking around, talking, falling over pews, sleeping on the pews, and arguing with each other with periodic outbreaks of violence.

Definitely a unique experience for Kathy and me, but in the midst of all this confusion we began to speak anyway.

At the end of the service, even though we figured no one had listened to us, we decided to give an altar call in hopes that maybe someone would come forward.

To our amazement so many people came forward that Kathy and I had to split up and form two separate prayer lines! As the people approached the alter, I asked each one what they wanted prayer for and one after another was in desperate need of a miracle of healing from God.

We prayed our hearts out for over two hours until every one who needed prayer had been prayed for.

To what result? Who knows!

Unfortunately, we never did see any obvious miracles and that upset me, so upon arriving back to the leadership, we shared with them what had happened, and how we had prayed and had seen no results.

Then a dear brother simply said, "All the Lord asks is that we be willing to pray, and then leave the results to Him." That was an important lesson for me; one (among others) which I would not have learned had I not been willing to stir up the gifts the Lord had given me: the gifts of Jesus, the Holy Spirit and the willingness to pray.

The point is that we must be willing to allow God to put us in situations where the gifts He has given us will be stirred up in spite of our feelings of fear or inadequacy.

Notice that I said that we are to allow God to create the circumstances and situations, not that we should get ourselves into these things without His direction! Many people have gotten hurt, become bitter and confused, because they were the ones who set up a situation and then asked God to show up and reap a victory for them.

I hope this will help those of you *who feel you have no gifts* to begin to examine the realities of what is going on in your life. God has given you the most precious gifts you'll ever have. It's simply your responsibility to learn how to "stir them up."

Another consideration of this concept is that all other gifts — such as those mentioned in I Corinthians 12 — are going to flow out of the gifts of Jesus Christ and the Holy Spirit.

Abuse of these gifts of God sometimes results in people pulling back from being used by God. These people will then offer examples to the Lord of "gift abuse" as their excuse for not stirring up their own gifts.

Abusing the privilege

Misuse of our gifts shows a problem at the source – perhaps a lack of depth or insensitivity to the leading of the Father. However, be aware of the fact that abuse of what the Lord has bestowed upon us is not God's "fault."

Instead, it is a failure on our part to recognize and in turn exercise, or stir up, that with which the Lord has endowed us.

I was in Norway speaking at a meeting with a couple of churches and as we were praising and worshipping the Lord a person spoke out with a tongue and it was interpreted.

I felt a questioning in my heart and wondered if it was really of the Lord.

We got back into the praise and worship, and another person spoke out in tongues with yet another interpretation.

Again I felt uneasy in my spirit.

But I said nothing.

Then, right in the middle of this person's interpretation someone else came out with another tongue.

I then realized what was going on was of the flesh, and not of the Spirit of God.

I quietly stepped up to the leader of this group and shared with him what I thought.

He turned to the pastor with whom I was staying and asked him what he felt.

The pastor said he agreed with me, and so we put a stop to the tongues and interpretations.

When I finally stood up to speak, I explained my actions to the audience, which included a very precious group of young people who God had mightily touched and brought out of the drug and alcohol scene.

Openness or abuse?

I told them that it was special to see their willingness to be open and to allow God's gifts to flow through them, and that it would certainly be advantageous to so many churches and groups in the body of Christ if they could be that open, too.

But I cautioned them that in their openness they needed to learn the fear of the Lord because it would be that fear which would keep them from speaking out in the flesh.

The leader received my remarks very well and the group as a whole also seemed receptive.

After the service, a brother came up to me and expressed how much he appreciated what had taken place.

He just wanted to encourage me that I had been correct in judging the tongues as not being of the Lord because he personally knew the people in this group and shared with me how many of them had truly been saved out of the drug and alcohol scene.

Unfortunately, there was still a lot of struggling with bitterness and resentment toward parents.

What happened was that they were basically being encouraged in self-acceptance through tongues and interpretation and, of course, that was opening the door for the enemy or the flesh to do the speaking, and not the Spirit of the Lord.

Practice, practice.

If you want to be good at something, it takes a lot of practice, which is precisely what Paul tells Timothy in verses 15 and 16.

"Practice these matters, devote yourself so that your advance may be evident to everyone. Look to yourself and to the teaching; keep right on in that, for in so doing, you will save yourself as well as your hearers."

The admonition here is to first practice these matters.

Which matters?

Basically everything that has been shared up to now: guarding against the fear of man, becoming an example before those who believe, continuing in the way, and not neglecting the gifts in you.

But being the lazy creatures we are, we simply figure that we're somehow going to grow up spiritually by osmosis!

Never!

So the encouragement to Timothy and us is to be thinking on these matters and working on them so their fruit will become more and more a natural part of our character.

Next Paul says to "look at yourself."

This is one of the very few times in the Bible when we are asked to do this, but the perspective here is to look at ourselves in the light of what we are speaking and teaching.

In other words, are we practicing what we preach?

Can others see that we live in accordance with what we speak or teach? This is what will attract others to listen to you – not how old you are, or how many books you have read, but rather the manifestation of a life being lived in harmony with what comes out of your mouth.

Timothy was a young man.

He had to learn, as we all must, how to minister to those who are both younger and older.

Paul speaks about this in I Timothy 5:1-2, "Do not rebuke an older man but plead with him as a father, and younger men as brothers, older women as mothers, and the younger women as sisters, with absolute purity." This simple principle was a tremendous help to me in my early days of counseling.

When the Lord began to lead me into counseling, I was 26 years old and single.

I have now been involved in counseling and ministering to the body of Christ for ten years and most of the people I see are older than me and married.

But in the beginning this was a bit of a threat until I realized that I was struggling with the fear of man and all I had to do was what Paul suggested to Timothy – treat older people with respect and younger people as I would a brother, and put my trust in the Lord who is able to meet their needs.

In I Timothy 6:11-12, Paul says, "But you, O man of God, shun these things and go after righteousness, godliness, faith, love, patience, gentleness.

"Fight the good fight of faith; take hold of the eternal life to which you were called as you made a good confession in the presence of many witnesses."

A man of God

We see that Paul referred to Timothy as a "man of God" and what we must realize is that He longs to call us all His men because He is no respecter of persons.

Therefore, the more we grow in the image of Christ, the more we become men and women of God.

Then Paul tells Timothy to "shun these things," which is a reference to the verses preceding I Timothy 6:11 in which we are asked to stay away from the love of money and to go after "righteousness, godliness, faith, love, patience, and gentleness," all of which are character traits of Christ.

As young men and women of God we are given specific direction which begins with an emphasis on our own character.

Allow God to deal with you.

Refusing to allow God to deal with our character flaws will hinder our spiritual growth and unless we humble ourselves, it will be impossible to establish the character of Jesus in our lives.

But when we allow God to deal with us in this way, He can begin to release more and more responsibility to us and we will continue to grow into greater spiritual maturity.

"... Fight the good fight of faith; take hold of the eternal life to which you were called as you made a good confession in the presence of many witnesses." This verse is actually an exciting challenge to us, with the concept of battle made very clear! As we began as babes in Christ, we must now look back on the importance of learning about "faith in God" as one of the elementary principles of Christ, a truth whose fruits we must exercise.

Very practically, friends, there are going to be many times, when in our walk with Jesus we will be called upon to fight the good fight of faith; but if there is no faith in God, there will be a lot of lost battles.

Later on in this chapter, I will be giving you a "Vision Chart" to provide you with specific examples of this concept of fighting the good fight of faith taking hold of eternal life and continuing in the way.

Now, let's look at another principle which Paul brings out in Timothy 6:20, "O Timothy, guard what has been entrusted to you.

"Keep away from irreligious and empty discussions and contradictions of what is falsely called knowledge which some people have claimed to have, and so have missed the mark with regard to the faith." In examining the first part of this verse, Paul speaks about guarding what has been given to us.

What an important principle this is, yet its neglect has been the downfall of so many of us! This concept of guarding is referring to how we are treating our relationship with Jesus and all He has given us.

The tendency in most relationships is to begin to take each other for granted, however, this is never the case with the Lord; He never takes us for granted.

But on the other hand, after we have walked with the Father for a while, it seems very easy for us to forget all that He has done for us and begin to allow other interests and affections take the place of that once-intense love for His presence.

The challenge?

The challenge here is to guard what we have been given in Christ.

Think about just what it is we have been given: everlasting life, forgiveness of sins, the fellowship of His presence, talents, abilities, anointings, callings, and so much more.

Have we been faithful to guard these things, or have we exposed the presence of the Lord to habitual sin and abuse in various ways? The Bible is very clear that if we remain faithful in a little, the Lord will give the increase.

Unfortunately, so many of us fail to protect what we have that we cause the Lord's hope and desire for us to be put on hold until we learn this simple but important principle.

Our prayer should be for revelation of just how much the Lord has bestowed upon us so our hearts will remain grateful and humble before Him.

I often wonder what has happened to so many young men and women of God as He began to raise them up in anointing and responsibility.

Some seemed to be walking in His anointing for a while, and then the next think you knew, they just weren't around any more.

I believe the failure of not properly guarding is why we often see God's anointing not lasting year in and year out on young men and women, and why as the scriptures say, there are just not many "fathers" or mature men of God.

Pointless debate.

The second part of I Timothy 6:20 says, "Keep away from irreligious and empty discussions and contradictions of what is falsely called knowledge, which some people have claimed to have, and so have missed the mark with regard to the faith." Having traveled fairly extensively, I find it interesting to note that almost all cultures worship knowledge as a "god" whether they seem to realize it or not.

That is why it is so easy for a Christian, in relation to God, to fall into the trap of finding and putting his security into head knowledge instead of faith.

Faith.

Again we come back to the very basic concept of learning to exercise our faith as babes in Christ so, as we grow, it will be faith in God that becomes our strength and leads us into the true knowledge of our heavenly Father.

As a young man or woman of God, it is important that we don't miss the mark with regard to the faith.

How is your faith doing? Has it suffered hurt, damage, misunderstandings, confusion and the like? The one thing we must always keep in mind is that God's ways are higher than ours and God's thoughts are higher than ours, and we can never afford to lose faith in Him no matter whether our intellect understands everything or not.

We can see in II Timothy 2:22

wherein Paul says, "But flee from the lusts of youth.

"Go in pursuit of integrity, faith, love, peace, in fellowship with those who call upon the Lord out of pure hearts."

Note the list.

In the second part of this verse, we have another practical list of character attributes of which, as young men and women of God, we should have a good understanding of each and how to grow in them.

But first, let's focus on the beginning of this verse where Paul says to Timothy to "flee from the lusts of youth." Our initial thought is that Paul is referring to sexual lusts, but that isn't the case.

The word "lust" is translated in Strong's Concordance as a "longing for what is forbidden," which is more than just a reference to sex.

So, let's figure out what it means.

It is quite typical for a young man of God to be highly motivated, zealous, ambitious, etc., which, if properly supervised and controlled, can result in great strides being realized for the Kingdom of God.

But it is also this highly-motivated zealousness that can get us into a lot of trouble and cause a good deal of confusion.

It is so easy for a young man of God to get carried away by a desire or ambition that just isn't of the Lord, no matter how noble it may seem.

Because some of our ideas seem so worthy, we must constantly be on guard to make sure we are aiming for the heart of God – for His vision for us – and not just longing for the fulfillment of a good idea.

Beware — deep hurt.

Failing to recognize these lusts of youth has resulted in deep hurt for so many young men and women of God, for which they often blame the Lord and their hearts turn bitter towards Him.

There are only two ways of responding when faced with this kind of hurt or misunderstanding.

First, there is the kind of response just mentioned wherein we begin to accuse God of not showing up and coming through for us when all we were trying to do was something for Him anyway.

This leads to self-justification and

then we begin to question God, become angry and bitter, and start pulling away from intimacy with Him.

Eventually our spirit begins to dry up, the joy of the Lord is gone, and we are obviously headed for some very hard times.

The second type of response is based on humility.

Humility.

Here we simply recognize that, although not intentional, a mistake has been made and it is certainly not God's fault.

We are aware that God is on our side, not holding anything against us, but desiring only to help.

Even though our intentions were pure, we recognize that our hurts were not brought upon us from God and so we humble ourselves, getting back on the right track with Him.

As we mature, we no longer get caught up in questioning the Lord's faithfulness and commitment to us.

In turn —

Nothing can shake our trust and commitment to Him.

Thus, in humility, we are brought back into the will of God without losing days, weeks, months, or years caught up in bitterness and self-justification.

An excellent example of this is seen in the life of King David.

David had a desire to build the Lord a temple, and certainly no one in the natural world would call that a selfish or evil desire.

Fortunately, David was a mature man of God and he took his desire before the Lord instead of just going ahead and following through on his own.

As David waited on the Lord, he heard Him say that it was not for David to do, but that it was for his son to build the temple.

A humble man of God.

Here we see the heart of a mature man of God.

Instead of feeling rejected and hurt, David simply did everything he could in humility to help his son build the temple.

Had David not laid his desire before the Lord, but gone ahead and built the temple, it would have carried with it certain repercussions because he would have been in disobedience.

Again the principle here is not

that we are to fear for our lives if we make a mistake, but to learn to walk in humility before the Lord, not allowing anything to rob us of our love and trust in Him.

The last area I would like to share with you has to do with the practical development of the call or vision of God in your life.

In Acts 2:17 it says,

"It will be in the last days, says God, that I shall pour out My spirit upon all flesh.

"Your sons and your daughters will prophesy and your youths will see visions ..."

Although I fully believe in the Lord giving visions to people, that is not what I am referring to here.

I'm referring to beginning to perceive and understand the vision which the Lord has for your own life as a young man or woman of God.

I remember during my early years on the mission field when other people would come up to me and ask what my vision in God was.

I always told them the same thing, "I just don't know." Many times, because of their response and my own insecurity, I would feel guilty and unspiritual for not knowing what the call of God was or what His vision was for my life.

As I have said, for the first three years I was on the mission field I did not know what I was going to be doing any further ahead than three months.

However, this kind of revelation was often looked upon as not being at all spiritual, especially by my pastor at that time and my friends back home, and at best, most of them looked at this kind of seemingly sporatic guidance as immaturity on my part. My point is that I was not being careless about seeking God for His call and vision in my life.

I had to find peace in the fact that I was being diligent and God gave me what He knew I could handle, and would give me more when He saw fit.

Let me give you some practical examples now from my own life in what I'm going to call the vision chart:

Vision Chart 1

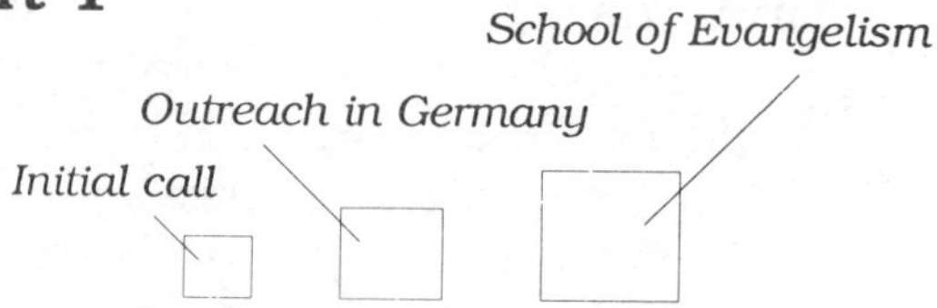

School of Evangelism

Outreach in Germany

Initial call

Never knowing what I was to do more than 3-6 months in advance.

In this first chart we see what we can refer to as the initial call of God.

In my case, the call was to go with Youth With A Mission (YWAM) to Europe.

There I went through my first training school.

It wasn't easy.

Just getting to the school involved overcoming some major obstacles such as we mentioned earlier.

Grace.

Only by the grace of God did I make it to and through that first school and accomplished what God had asked me to do.

At the end of school, I sought the Lord.

I asked: What do I do next?

He lead me to join the YWAM staff in Hawaii.

What an assignment!

A missionary in Paradise!

It was there that I was asked to go with another young man throughout New Zealand and the Pacific, finally ending up on Guam to help head up the South Pacific games.

Vision Chart 2

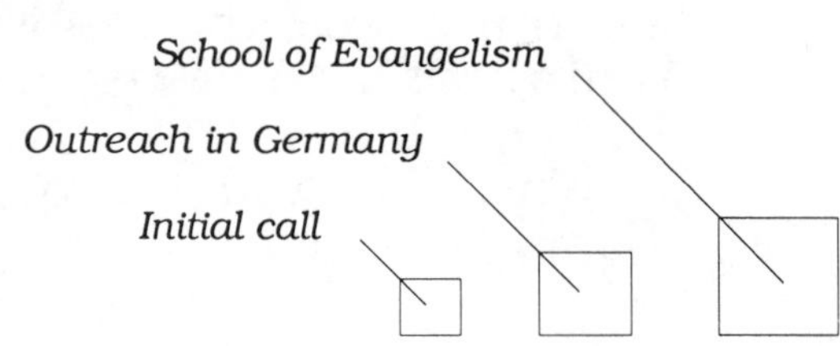

Just getting to Hawaii was difficult, and so was what I was now being asked to do.

I remember going to the airport in Los Angeles, knowing I was $20 short of the airfare to Hawaii.

I had heard all these stories about angels showing up and providing His children with money in situations just like this.

So, I arrived truly expecting an angel to come to my rescue.

At the airport, I got in line to purchase my ticket.

I got all the way to the counter and –

There was no angel.

So I went and sat down, figuring I needed to give my angel more time to get to where I was.

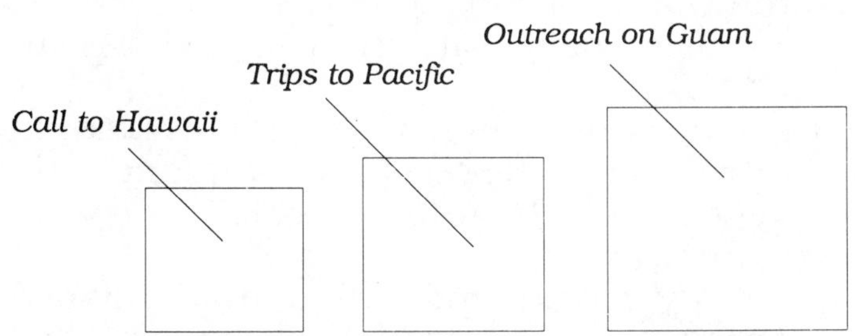

Still never knowing what I was to do 6-8 months in advance.

As I was sitting there, a young man who had come in on the same bus with me approached me and said, "I don't understand this, but I am feeling compelled to give you a $20 bill."

Well, this just made my day!

I told the young man my situation, thanked him and the Lord for His faithfulness to me, and knew I was on my way. I purchased my ticket and made it to Hawaii with only a few pennies left in my pocket.

But this was a different matter.

Now the leadership was asking me to fly to New Zealand and all over the Pacific to help lead an outreach on Guam.

It was definitely overwhelming, but in obedience to the Lord, I began to walk it out.

The next situation came up in New Zealand.

It was the last day I could purchase a ticket to Guam and still keep the schedule to which we were committed.

My friend and I had just finished speaking at a small Bible school and we were getting into our car to leave when the president of the school came out and called us into his office.

He asked us if we had all our finances for the trip to Guam, to which my friend replied, "Yes." I, however, was $350 short.

This loving gentleman then proceeded to open up his desk drawer, pulled out his check book, and wrote me a check in that exact amount!

What an answer to prayer!

He said he believed we were doing what the Lord had asked of us and prayed a blessing on us.

Rejoicing in the Lord, we excitedly drove to the travel agent, arriving just before closing time and purchased the tickets.

The next day we were off to our

destination via many of the South Pacific islands where we had an opportunity to share our vision of the new outreach for Guam.

We had been given the name of the local pastor, the Rev. John Burke and upon arrival, called him.

After telling John of our situation, he graciously provided housing for us during our entire stay on Guam.

As the months before the outreach went by, we secured an elementary school to house everyone coming for the event.

Everything seemed set.

Then, something rather "typical" happened.

The day before the outreach was to begin, the local Board of Education came to us and informed us that we could no longer stay in their facility.

This was an obvious attack by the enemy in an attempt to thwart the good that was to be done.

What could we do?

My friend Kelvin went to discuss the matter with the education people while I gathered all those who had just flown in and told them that if we were going to have an outreach, we

Vision Chart 3

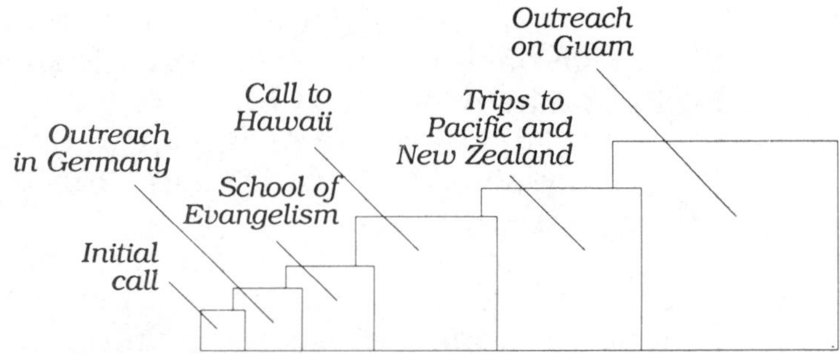

Each call was larger and carried more responsibility than before.

were going to have to "fight the good fight of faith!" Of course, this is the same principle which Paul spoke of to Timothy.

And so we began to pray and late in the afternoon, Kelvin came back and reported to us that we could stay the night but would have to leave the next day.

This cycle went on for three days.

Then it broke and we were given permission to stay there for the entire outreach.

Then, an interesting thing happened.

We had wondered how we would

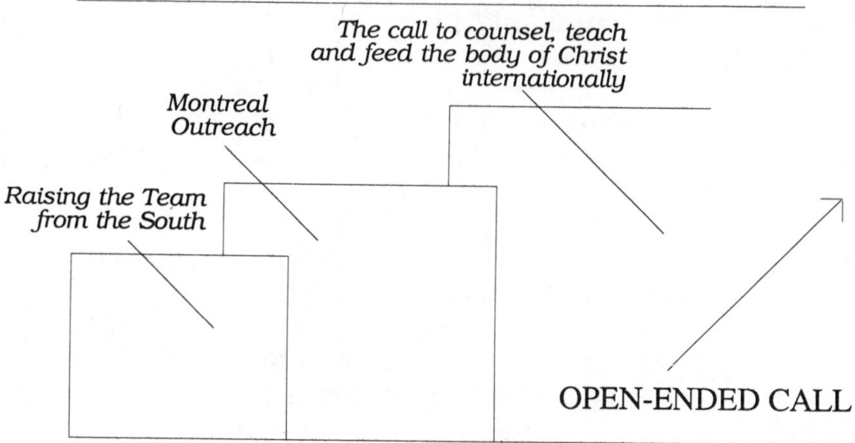

The Lord was now revealing what he wanted me to do up to a year in advance

ever get such a diversified group of people into a place of unity so we might have an effective outreach.

Well, what the enemy had planned as destruction for us was turned to our good by the Lord.

At the end of those three days of prayer, we were the most unified group you could ever hope to see!

Consequently —

We had a powerful outreach and the work on Guam still goes on today, 12 years later.

As my time on Guam drew to a close, I was seeking the Lord as to what He would have me do next.

I didn't expect the answer.

I felt lead to go home and raise up a team of young people from the South and take them to the Olympic Games in Montreal.

Well, I argued with the Lord about that for a while because I didn't want to do what I believed He was asking.

But after accepting it in my heart, I submitted it to leadership and they believed it was right for me to do also, and so I began to walk it out.

This simple but often difficult principle of walking out what the Lord has said is very important in realizing the fulfillment of everything the Lord has planned for each of us.

Walking in faith.

As I stepped out in faith in the direction the Lord had indicated, He opened many doors for me in different southern states.

Then the next thing I knew, I had a team and off we went, bound for the Olympic Games in Montreal.

The accomplishment of the Lord's work took about one year, but everything He had said came to pass as I was faithful and trusted Him, and walked in obedience.

Our time at the Olympics was tremendous for the entire team and many stayed permanently with YWAM after the games were over.

Waiting, seeking

But again I found myself seeking the Lord's guidance for what I should be doing next.

As I waited on Him I believed He was asking me to go into counseling.

I already had a degree in psychology and had often wondered if I would ever go further into this field.

The immediate problem seemed to be that YWAM didn't have any opportunities open for a full-time counseling ministry even though almost everything they did involved some kind of counseling.

But I still felt the Lord was telling me to go into this as a full-time venture, so I figured I would have to leave YWAM.

An unexpected answer:

Well, the very next morning at a general meeting before we left Montreal, Loren Cunningham, the International Director for YWAM, stood up and said, "By the way, there is going to be a doctor from New

Vision Chart 4

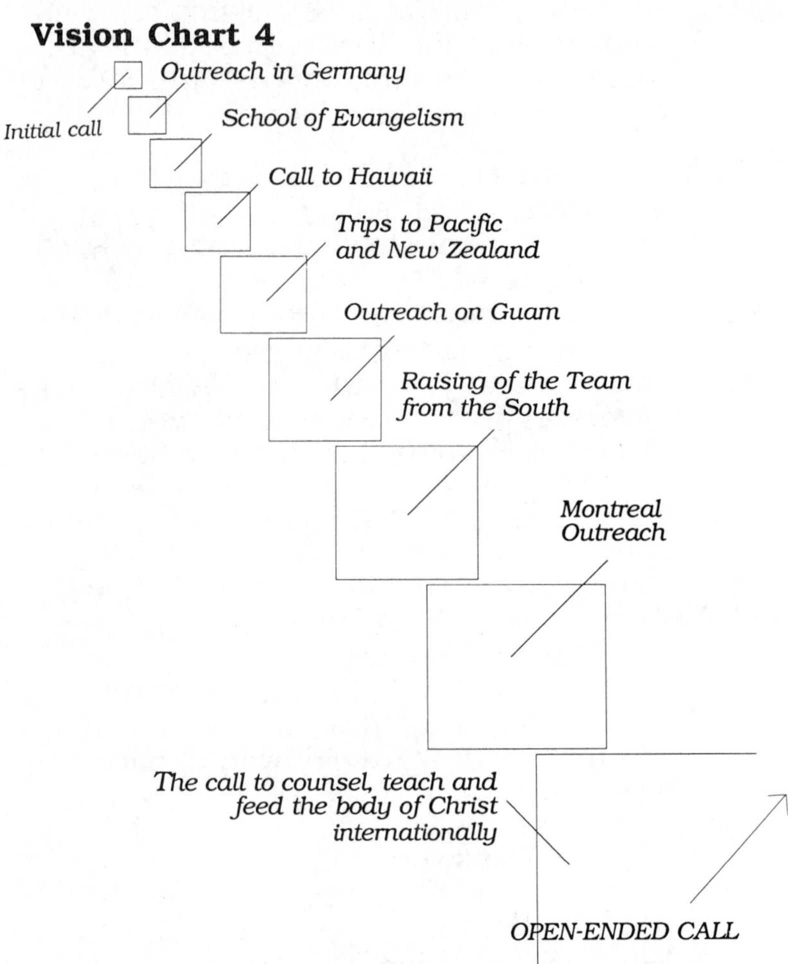

It is "normal" to go as long as 3 years and only be aware of His plan in 3- to 6-month increments.

Zealand joining Youth With A Mission and he is going to start a family counseling ministry in Hawaii and is in need of staff help." I couldn't believe my ears! Just the night before, the Lord had put this very thing on my heart.

So I went to Loren and shared with him what I was feeling and he arranged for me to meet Dr. Bruce Thompson.

Dr. Bruce and I met and as we prayed together we both felt that it was right for me to come and join him in Hawaii to assist in the establishment of the first family counseling ministry for YWAM.

As you can see —

This time the Lord's call was left open-ended.

Previously, His calls always had a time limit set on them, whether it was as little as three months or as long as one year.

But each was very important in its own right as a step of obedience leading to what I believe is now a major call of God on my life.

I believe the reason this call was left open-ended is because God is adding to it all the time, and again, the key seems to be obedience.

Let's look at the final chart again.

As you can see, before I received what I considered a definite call from God, about three very important years of testing went by enabling the Lord to lay a proper and solid foundation upon which He could continue to build His will.

As you look at the chart:

Let me ask you, What do you think is the most critical point on the whole chart? If the very beginning is your answer, you are exactly right! Friends, it is during the very beginning of our walk with God that we are the most vulnerable to being sidetracked by the enemy and when that happens, we may never realize all the good that the Lord had planned for us.

This is why we are never to take lightly the calls of God on our life, but walk them out in all diligence and obedience.

The truth is —

The truth is, I am still seeking to do this today in following that call which is still open-ended.

God will always keep visions and goals in front of us as we seek to obey

Him and it is very typical that each goal and each vision He places before us will be larger than the one before.

Thus we should allow ourselves to be stretched and challenged – seemingly beyond our abilities – but always within His reach!

Mature in God

As we delve deeper into the biblical concepts of maturity, I want you to realize that these are shared in order to excite and challenge your hearts as to what lies ahead for you as you grow up toward Him who is the Head.

From previous chapters, it is obvious that even though in some ways we may be functioning as young men and women of God, in other ways we may still be struggling with some of the difficulties of being a babe or child.

Please understand that —

This is normal and one of the purposes of this book is to help each of us see where we are in God's family — both where we are doing well and where we need work.

Let's look at I John 2:14-15, "I have written you, fathers, because you have learned to know Him who is from the beginning ... Neither love the world nor the things in the world.

Whoever loves the world has not the Father's love in his heart."

The first key point here is that the mature man "knows" God.

He knows the Father.

This is not just a casual acquaintance or an emphasis on head knowledge, but the intimate, heartfelt knowledge that is born out of following the footsteps of Jesus and knowing what it means to fellowship in the sufferings of Christ.

Because the mature have come to know God, they have an understanding of His will for their lives, and therefore, they have a sense of security as to where they fit into His kingdom.

This is not meant to imply, however, that the mature are not still growing in their understanding – because they are. But they are not anxious when those growth times are upon them, rather they go through these difficulties with an assurance and a peace in God.

It is a characteristic of the mature not to be enticed by the things of the world, but to relate to the world out of the Father's love.

Paul mentions that he had learned to be satisfied both in abundance and in need and so must we – as we grow – not be tempted by what the world has to offer us, but *rather learn to be content* at each level of spiritual maturity.

Learning this contentment means never allowing the things of the world and its temptations to ever take the place of following God in His will for our lives.

Here's a very practical example:

Let me share with you a very practical example.

Having been closely involved with large numbers of people going out into the mission field, I find there are usually two common responses when it comes to leaving behind the things of the world.

The first response involves struggles with God's call which can last for weeks or even months.

In reality, this struggle is usually not that they haven't heard God's call, but rather with leaving behind the things of the world, whether those things be material, or friendships, or special relationships.

An attitude of humility

The second response is one of humility – where the attitude taken is that it is a privilege to have been called, and therefore a privilege to give up certain things.

Whether or not we ever go to the mission field, we must maintain this attitude of humility to protect ourselves from being bound or limited by material possessions, friendships, or special relationships, thereby keeping us from responding to God's will in our lives.

There are a number of important principles to be drawn from John 15:14–16.

"You are My friends if you do what I command you. I no longer call you slaves, for a slave does not know what his master is doing, but I have called you friends because I have acquainted you with everything I heard from My Father. You have not chosen Me, but I have chosen you and appointed you to go out and produce fruit and that your fruit should be permanent, so that whatever you ask the Father in My name He may grant you."

Let's look at verse 16 wherein we can identify four main characteristics of the mature:

First:

"I have chosen you ..." – It is vital that we know we have been specifically chosen to accomplish certain tasks for the Lord.

Thus, like Paul who said he was "compelled to preach the gospel," as we mature, we know we are chosen and are compelled to be about what God has asked us to do.

Second:

"... appointed you to go out ..." – Along with knowing they are chosen, the mature recognize the appointing from the Lord to go out and accomplish that which He has laid on their hearts.

It is this commission that is so important and which leads to the anointing of God as we walk in obedience.

Third:

"... and produce fruit ..." – One of the key marks of having been chosen and appointed by God will be an evidence of fruit; not in our own eyes, but in the eyes of others.

Thus it is normal for the mature to be producing fruit.

Fourth:

"... your fruit should be permanent ..." – It is not enough for us, as we mature, to simply produce fruit.

It should be our desire that whatever is produced will remain permanent.

We see this same characteristic in the life of Jesus when He was talking to the Father and said He had not lost any of those the Father had given Him except Judas.

Today there are many men of God who believe they are chosen and appointed to go out and produce fruit, but without any true concern for permanency.

Until their hearts long for this characteristic, they will continue to miss the mark and example of maturity set by Jesus.

Let's examine verses 14 and 15.

Let's picture the situation as Jesus was walking and talking to his disciples, trying to bring to their attention an acknowledgment of spiritual maturity.

In order to do this, Jesus was using the example of the difference between a slave and a friend.

Now remember these two words – slave and friend – have nothing to do with Jesus' love changing toward His disciples.

He is using these words as an example of spiritual maturity.

Moms, dads and kids.

A practical example of this would be the relationship between parents and their child.

The parents love the child when it is young and they continue to love the child when it is older.

But as the child matures, there comes a natural change in its relationship with the parents whereby the child's growth and maturity are acknowledged.

The disciples' relationship with Jesus was no longer the same and He was trying to bring that to their attention.

So Jesus said,

"I no longer call you slaves, for a slave does not know what his master is doing ..." There was a time when

Jesus was frequently having to explain everything to His disciples.

Have you ever been in a situation where you wanted to share what was on your heart, but you knew there just wasn't anyone around that would completely understand even if you tried to explain it to them? Well, this is what Jesus put up with for a long time.

There were certain things He longed to tell His disciples but He knew they were not yet capable of understanding.

Slaves and masters.

This is what Jesus meant when He used the concept of a slave not knowing what his master is doing.

We can realize then, just how excited Jesus must have been to at last be giving His disciples an acknowledgment of spiritual maturity.

The principle of using the word "friend" is a precious one; as His disciples walked faithfully with Him, Jesus called them into an even deeper relationship.

He called them to come alongside of Him where He said He would make known to them everything He had heard from the Father.

What an incredible concept to see the heart of Jesus longing to share everything with the disciples! What an awesome place of accountability and responsibility – the place of maturity!

Let's see how this principle affected the life of Moses.

In Psalm 103:7, it says,

"He revealed His ways to Moses, His dealings to the people of Israel." Here we see this principle in the life of Moses and what it can mean to the body of Christ.

As Moses drew near to the Lord, He revealed His ways to him, and as Moses grew in understanding these ways, the dealings of the Lord were revealed to the children of Israel.

We see that because of one mature man drawing near to God, thousands of people were actually blessed.

It's no wonder we should be praying for God to raise up mature men and women in our churches because an entire nation can be greatly blessed and influenced by the dealings of God simply because one mature man or woman drew near to the Father.

Understanding the times and the way the body is to go:

In I Chronicles 12:32, we are told, "... 200 of their leaders who had understanding of the times and knew what Israel should do ..." This gives us two very important principles which are to be embraced by true leaders and/or the mature.

The first portion of this concept is understanding the times.

An understanding of the times

A mature man of God will have an understanding of the times which comes not from the evening news on TV, but from having drawn near the Father and having received wisdom from the Spirit.

I remember once when I was traveling with a precious couple, Ken and Shirley Wright.

A visit to Africa

We were scheduled to fly to Rhodesia for a time of ministry just after the elections had been concluded.

Mugabee, a Marxist, had won, sending the country into temporary unrest, and we were told to wait and see if the country would close its borders.

After several days we were given

permission to fly in and proceed with our meetings.

Upon arrival, it was apparent that the body of Christ there was in a turmoil.

They couldn't understand why God had allowed a Marxist to be elected and they were confused about their own safety and what they were to do next.

We are to trust, not fear.

Into this situation Ken began to speak "understanding of the times." I remember he told them they were misinterpreting what God was about.

He told them that God had allowed that man to be elected in order to spare thousands of lives that would have been lost had he not been elected, because Mugabee had a tremendous amount of political force behind him.

For example, we were told stories of how Mugabee's troops came into a village, made all the people stand in line, and then had one of the young men step forward shooting him on the spot.

Afterward they told the people if they didn't vote for Mugabee they would be back to destroy the village.

We personally stayed in the home of a couple whose house came under attack one night and the mother ran back into the bedroom to get the children just as a rifle grenade came through the window.

The curtain miraculously blew upwards and caught the grenade, wrapping tightly around it so it never went off.

The hand of God.

There were many true stories of how the hand of God wrought miracles during all the fighting that took place and have been compiled into a small book entitled God in Rhodesia.

So here was Ken, giving the body of Christ understanding that had come from being in the presence of God.

God — still on his throne.

I can still remember how he admonished them not to forget that God was still on the throne and to be about the task of saving souls while there was still time.

How critically important it is for the leadership of the church to have an understanding of the times, gaining spiritual discernment from the Father's perspective into what is going on in their own churches.

Knowing the way

The second concept mentioned in I Chronicles 12:32 is that the leaders "knew what Israel should do." Thus we realize yet another important characteristic of the mature: knowng the way the flock should go.

This has to do with understanding God's vision and direction for the flock and the work to which He has called the church.

It is unfortunate to see how much deception abounds when it comes to pastors and leaders understanding God's vision and direction for the church, and having to set aside their own individual desires and visions.

I wonder what would happen if Jesus showed up in all the churches of our land and asked each congregation a simple question:

"What is the vision of this church?"

What kind of answer do you suppose He would get?

My guess is that the vast majority would have no real answer because most of those in leadership are "too busy" to spend enough time alone with God to get His vision.

It is extremely sad to think that all the vision and direction most churches have today is building a bigger or another building.

Both of these concepts – understanding the times according to God and knowing the way the flock is to go – are key elements in the character traits of the mature Christian.

Whether you are leading a Sunday school class, a youth group, an outreach group, a church, or are involved in a personal ministry, you should be putting these principles into practice, staying before the Lord to obtain wisdom and understanding from His perspective for your particular leadership situation.

Ministry unto the Lord.

In Ezekiel 44, the Lord is talking about Israel and the Levites, the tribe chosen to be priests who ministered to the Lord.

In this chapter, the Lord brings out two major areas of failure which apply not only to the Levites, but also to those pastors and leaders who are in positions of authority today.

The first accusation is found in

verse 8, "You have not kept proper charge of My holy things, but you have appointed for yourselves keepers to take charge of My sanctuary." Today we are seeing this same mistake being made because pastors and church leaders are still not taking proper care of the "holy things," that is, the body of Christ.

It is in verse 12 that we see what it is the Levites were doing wrong.

"But because the Levites ministered to the people before their gods and thereby became a stumbling block of inquity to the house of Israel, therefore I have sworn with uplifted hand concerning them, says the Lord God, that they shall bear their punishment."

Their punishment is in this verse:

"They shall not come near Me to minister as priests to Me or to touch any of My sacred things, but they shall bear their shame because of the abominations which they have committed."

We must realize the severity of what the Lord is saying to the leaders.

First of all, we see them not taking proper care of the body of Christ.

Instead, they were actually ministering first to the people instead of to God.

The consequence of this results in God not allowing them to come near Him and minister to Him.

This is so typical of what many pastors and church leaders are caught up in today because of preconceived denominational traditions and expectations.

Instead of drawing near and ministering first to the Lord, they are caught in a vicious cycle of trying to minister to the wills and demands of the people.

The unfortunate thing about this is:

It is precisely the role model we have grown to expect of a pastor – and sadly, thousands of them have fallen right into the trap of running around trying to meet the wills and demands of the people instead of learning to minister to the Lord first!

Many people in the church look on and call this kind of activity "spiritual."

But, the Lord looks on it and says it is an abomination because it is nothing more than fear of man! What has actually happened is that falling into the trap of the system, pastors have established their own congregations as false idols which they run around and serve even unto death.

Statistics show that pastors have the second highest coronary rate of any profession and it comes as a direct consequence of following the people and ministering to their desires, which if seen for what it is, would be called idolatry. I realize this is a heavy indictment, but idolatry is a serious reality and look at the drastic punishment ... "they shall not come near Me to minister as priests to Me ... "

Look also at Jesus' life and example:

He continuously had needs pressing in on Him, yet what was His single most guiding factor? It was as He said in John 4:34, "My nourishment is that I do the will of Him who sent Me and completely do His work." Jesus was the most compassionate person ever, yet He was never lead, guided or dictated to by the needs and demands of people, but rather only by the will of the Father.

Although the needs and demands of people are certainly real, they are never to be our guiding factor.

We must never minister to people first, thinking the Lord will accept time left over as ministry unto Him.

There is a verse in Philippians 2:21 which says, "They are all looking out for their interests, not for those of Christ Jesus." Tragically, when leadership (consciously or not) puts the desires of the people first, this is exactly what happens, and the interests of Jesus come after the interests of the people. One strong reason for leaders moving in this area of deception is that their salary is drawn from the people. Thus the thought of how they may be moving in the fear of man never crosses their mind. Self-justification comes so easy.

To expose this abomination of the heart, one must cry out to God for His conviction upon them where they may be moving in the fear of man-idolatry — and be willing to pay the price of then walking in the fear of the Lord. As we return to Ezekiel 44, we read in verses 15 and 16 about the blessings of those who walk in the fear of the Lord, "But the Levitical priests, the sons of Zadok, who kept the charge of My sanctuary when the children of Israel went astray from Me, they shall come near to Me to minister to Me, and they shall stand before Me to offer to Me the fat and the blood, says the Lord God; they shall enter My sanctuary, and they shall come near to My table to minister to Me, and they shall keep My charge." You see, mature men of God take proper care of the body of Christ.

They will draw near and learn to minister to God, and as a result, the Lord will allow them, as true shepherds, to minister to the people with His anointing. As you draw near and minister to the Lord first, the true needs of the people will be met due to the Lord's compassion and faithfulness being released because of your obedience to minister first to Him.

How marvelous is the simple truth of God which always sets us free!

I have traveled extensively sharing this message, and it is at this point that I would like to encourage those of you who recognize that you have been caught up in idolatry and the fear of man, to humble yourselves before God and repent. I have seen many pastors and church leaders, and thus congregations, come into a new place in God as they have faced and repented of what has been going on in their ministry to the body of Christ.

I'm reminded of II Corinthians 7:10: "For the sorrow that God approves works out a repentance that leads to salvation such as is never regretted, while the world's sorrow produces death." What is needed here is godly sorrow for having moved in idolatry and fear of man.

The fellowship of Christ's sufferings

As we look into this area of the sufferings of Christ and how they apply to the mature, I would like to share three scriptures.

The first is II Corinthians 6:4–10, "Rather, we prove ourselves in every respect as servants of God, by great endurance, in afflictions, distresses, and hardships; in lashes, imprisonments, and disturbances; in toils, sleepless nights, and without food; through purity, knowledge, and endurance of wrongs; through kindness, by the Holy Spirit, in genuine love; with a message of truth, by the power of God; by means of the weapons of righteousness for attack and defense; through honor and shame; through blame and praise; considered imposters when we are honest, and unknown when we are well known; thought of as dying when, you see, we are alive, and as disciplined but not put to death; as deceived and yet always joyful; as poor but making many wealthy; as having nothing and yet in possession of everything."

Let me note two things about this:

Note that this is a practical list of how the disciples proved themselves as God's servants. How many of these things can you identify with, and how have you handled each one of these areas in your own life and walk with the Lord? We have all gone through at least one of these areas, and most of us probably got upset with the Lord for "allowing" it to happen to us.

Did we equate what we went through as the fellowship of His sufferings, and as the way we must prove ourselves as servants of the living God just as the disciples did?

The second scripture is Philippians 3:10 and 15, "That I may know Him, and the power of His resurrection and the sharing of His sufferings, becoming like Him in His death ... Let those of us, then, who are mature have this in mind, and if your views differ in any respect, God will make this clear also to you." It seems the body of Christ has gotten to the point where the word "suffering" is looked upon as a bad word, mainly because of misguided modern teachings ignoring the sufferings of Christ and how they apply to the Christian. Instead of being afraid of the concept of Christ's sufferings, we should cultivate this same perspective as taught by the disciples in I Peter 4:1, "Since Christ, then, has suffered physically, you also must arm yourselves with the same attitude ..." and in Philippians 1:29: "For you have been privileged on behalf of Christ not only to believe in Him but also to suffer for Him ... "

We must arm ourselves with the reality that Jesus suffered for us and there may be times when, in our service to Him, we also will incur some suffering. These verses speak to us regarding the perspective with which we are to look upon these times;not as hardships, but as a privilege, as we are taught by the disciples.

How does that compare with your perspective on Christ's sufferings? What we begin to realize here is: the mature man of God is acquainted with sufferings and *is not afraid of them* because we realize that the sufferings of Christ are a chosen suffering.

All of the disciples chose to follow

Jesus, and as a result, travailed in many ways, some even unto death. But it was a chosen suffering out of their love and commitment to the Lord.

Have you chosen to follow Jesus? How is your fellowship with His sufferings doing in such practical areas as your job, your family, your life? You see, friends, your maturity or lack of it will show when the practical sufferings of Christ come your way.

It's interesting that in spite of all the disciples went through, their attitude could be summed up in Paul's statement, "I count it all joy."

Dear friends, we are never to fear the fellowship of His sufferings. Instead, we are to grow in maturity with the examples and attitudes taught us by the disciples.

There have been times in my own life when my immaturity showed while walking through some of the fellowship of His sufferings. I, too, am working on these principles of maturity just as I am encouraging you to work them into your life.

"Until we all may arrive at the unity of faith and that understanding of that Son of God that brings completeness of personality, tending toward the measure of the stature of the fullness of Christ." In many ways, Ephesians 4:13 captures what we have been about throughout this book.

Understand it isn't that you are only functioning in one of these areas of maturity or the other. It is more likely that in some areas of your life, you will recognize traits of a babe – and in others traits of a young adult. It is our maturing in the Lord that bring abouts a completeness of our personality and a stability in our walk with the Lord. I trust, as you go through each level of spiritual maturity, you will be able to understand where you fit into God's family, and what needs to take place in your life to continue growing. I hope God has ministered to you and His ministry will consistently produce permanent fruit in your life. In closing, I would like to relate a true story that has meant so much to me.

It was shared by my friend Ken Wright and revolves around I Corinthians 1:9, "God is trustworthy, through Whom you were called into the companionship of His Son, our Lord Jesus Christ." One day a local pastor was reading this verse and felt convicted that he had not properly responded to the Lord's call to companionship or fellowship with Himself.

So in his heart he was determined to start spending special time just giving himself to the Lord. He would go and sit in his favorite chair and just be with God. As the pastor was meditating, Jesus appeared before him.

The pastor just sat there waiting to see what our Lord was going to do.

As he remained quiet, Jesus came over to where he was sitting, went around and stood behind him. Then the pastor began to feel what he thought were drops of rain on his head, but he realized they were the tears of Jesus. Then, he heard the Lord speak: "My son, you have no idea how much I love your presence."

Oh, how true this is!

We have no idea how much the Lord loves our presence, but the truth is: we have been called into the fellowship or companionship of His Son.

When I heard this story, I thought about one of the principles set forth in Ezekiel. As the mature, we are to learn to minister to the Lord. I think the best way to answer this question is to ask another. How has the Lord chosen to give Himself or minister to you? The simple and obvious answer is by His time or Himself. This is actually the way we begin to learn to minister to the Lord ... by giving Him ourselves and our time. This should involve both a special time alone with Him and a natural relating to God in all we do throughout the day.

So, like this pastor,

We must recognize that we have been called to fellowship with Jesus. The best way to begin doing that is to start setting aside time alone, giving yourself to the Lord.

As King David meditated in His presence, dear friends, we, too, are likewise called into his fellowship.

Thus, responding to His call and learning to minister unto God simply becomes a priority and a lifestyle for the mature.

But the call is for the entire body of Christ.

I trust you now have a better perspective on where you are fitting into the family of God from these principles we have shared on spiritual maturity.

Jesus is waiting for you.

He loves your presence.

Why not go to Him now?

Also Available

These spirit-filled teachings are available from:

STEVE SHAMBLIN
4120 White Pine Drive
Raleigh, NC 27612

Cassette tapes are $6.50, including postage and handling. Video cassettes are $54.95 each, postage and handling included. Personal checks, money orders and cashier checks acceptable.

How to Grow Up Spiritually

A 4-part series looking at character traits of a babe, child, young adult and mature man or woman of God.

A Christian Identity Series

A 3-part series on Our Christian Identity, Acceptance and Rejection, and Concepts of Wounded Spirit.

Marriage

A 4-part series looking at the Marriage Covenant, Basis for Marriage,

Roles of Husband and Wife, Emotional Differences Between Male and Female.

Counseling

A 2-part series looking at "spiritual tools" the Lord has given us for ministry into the lives of other people.

Fear of Man Series

A 2-part series exposing the bondage related to the fear of man.

Individual Cassette Messages

Fear of the Lord	Obedience
Hunger After God	Intercession
Spiritual Authority	Guidance
Abiding in Christ	Holiness

Priorities in Relationships
Fear and Emotional Repression
An Ungrateful Spirit
The Blessings of Endurance

Abiding in Christ

A 60-minute video teaching us the value of waiting on the Lord.

Christian Identity Series

Video series contains three 90-minute messages on our Identity, Acceptance, Rejection and the Wounded Spirit. (Tapes can be purchased separately, but we encourage purchase of the entire series since the platform is built from one message to the other.)

Faith-Building Books From Huntington House

America Betrayed! by Marlin Maddoux. This hard-hitting book exposes the forces in our country which seek to destroy the family, the schools and our values. This book details exactly how the news media manipulates your mind. Marlin Maddoux is the host of the popular, national radio talk show "Point of View."

A Reasonable Reason to Wait, by Jacob Aranza, is a frank, definitive discussion on premarital sex — from the biblical viewpoint. God speaks about premarital sex, according to the author. The Bible also provides a healing message for those who have been sexually involved before marriage. This book is a must reading for every young person — and also for parents — who really want to know the biblical truth on this important subject.

Backward Masking Unmasked, by Jacob Aranza. Rock'n'Roll music affects tens of millions of young people and adults in America and around the world. This music is laced with lyrics exalting drugs, the occult, immorality, homosexuality, violence and rebellion. But there is a more sinister danger in this music, according to the author. It's called "backward masking." Numerous rock groups employ this mind-influencing technique in their recordings. Teenagers by the millions — who spend hours each day listening to rock music — aren't even aware the messages are there. The author clearly exposes these dangers.

Backward Masking Unmasked, (cassette tape) by Jacob Aranza. Hear actual satanic messages and judge for yourself.

Computers and the Beast of Revelation, by Dr. David Webber and Noah Hutchings. The authors masterfully explain the arrival of this great age of information, particularly relating to computers, in light of Bible prophecy. They share information about computer control, computer networks, computer spies and the ultimate computer. Today there are signs all around us that computers are merging all economic transactions into a single, all-knowledgeable system and all nations into one economic system. For centuries Bible scholars have wondered how Revelation 13 could ever be fulfilled: When would some kind of image or machine command everyone in the world to work or buy and sell with code marks and numbers? This book answers that question.

Devil Take the Youngest by Winkie Pratney. This book reveals the war on children that is being waged in America and the world today. Pratney, a world-renowned author, teacher and conference speaker, says there is a spirit of Moloch loose in the land. The author relates distinct parallels of the ancient worship of Moloch, where little children were sacrificed screaming into his burning fire, to the tragic killing and kidnapping of children today. This timely book says the war on children has its roots in the occult.

Globalism: America's Demise, by William Bowen, Jr. The Globalists — some of the most powerful people on earth — have plans to totally eliminate God, the family, and the United States as we know it today. Globalism is the vehicle the humanists are using to implement their secular humanistic philosophy to bring about their one-world government. The four goals of Globalism are: 1) a one-world government; 2) a new world religion; 3) a new economic system; 4) a new race of people for the new world order. This book alerts Christians to what Globalists have planned for them.

How to Cope When You Can't by Don Gossett is a guide to dealing with the everyday stresses and pressures of life. Gossett, a well-known Christian author and evangelist, draws from many personal experiences in this book which brings hope and encouragement for victory in our Lord. The author deals with such contemporary subjects as coping with guilt, raising children, financial difficulties, poverty, a sectarian spirit, the devil's devices, pride, fear and inadequacy, sickness, sorrow, enemies and other real problems. This book is a must for Christians who want to be victorious.

More Rock, Country & Backward Masking Unmasked by Jacob Aranza. Aranza's first book, *Backward Masking Unmasked* was a national bestseller. It clearly exposed the backward satanic messages included in a lot of rock and roll music. Now, in the sequel, Aranza gives new information on backward messages. For the first time, he takes a hard look at the content, meaning and dangers of country music. "Rock, though filled with satanism, sex and drugs ... has a hard time keeping up with the cheatin', drinkin' and one-night stands that continue to dominate country music," the author says.

Murdered Heiress ... Living Witness, by Dr. Petti Wagner. The victim of a sinister kidnapping and murder plot, the Lord miraculously gave her life back to her. Dr. Wagner — heiress to a large fortune — was kidnapped, tortured, beaten, electrocuted and died. A doctor signed her death certificate, yet she lives today!

Rest From the Quest, by Elissa Lindsey McClain. This is the candid account of a former New Ager who spent the first 29 years of her life in the New Age Movement, the occult and Eastern mysticism. This is an incredible inside look at what really goes on in the New Age Movement.

The Divine Connection, by Dr. Donald Whitaker. This is a Christian guide of life extension. It specifies biblical principles on how to feel better and live longer and shows you how to experience Divine health, a happier life, relief from stress, a better appearance, a healthier outlook on life, a zest for living and a sound emotional life.

The Great Falling Away Today, by Milton Green. This renowned speaker shows the joy and peace that comes through deliverance — and cites what the Bible says about the future of an unrepentant church.

The Hidden Dangers of the Rainbow, by Constance Cumbey. A national #1 bestseller, this is a vivid exposé of the New Age Movement which she says is dedicated to wiping out Christianity and establishing a one-world order. This movement, a vast network of occult and other organizations, meets the test of prophecy of the Antichrist.

The Hidden Dangers of the Rainbow Tape, by Constance Cumbey. Mrs. Cumbey, a trial lawyer from Detroit, Michigan, gives inside information on the New Age Movement in this teaching tape.

The Twisted Cross, by Joseph Carr. One of the most important works of our decade, *The Twisted Cross* clearly documents the occult and demonic influence on Adolf Hitler and the Third Reich which led to the killing of more than 6 million Jews. The author even gives specifics of the bizarre way in which Hitler actually became demon-possessed.

Where Were You When I Was Hurting? by Nicky Cruz. Former New York City teen gang leader Nicky Cruz takes the reader on a gripping, emotion-packed trek into earthquake-shattered Mexico City, into drug-plagued Budapest, Hungary, into Satanist-infested Asuncion, Paraguay, South America, and back into the streets of New York and Chicago with the message of God's healing that comes when we are willing to give up our bitterness and simply forgive. A powerful teaching and witnessing tool from one of America's all-time bestselling authors.

Who Will Rise Up? by Jed Smock. This is the incred ible — and sometimes hilarious — story of Jed Smock, who with his wife, Cindy, has preached the uncompromising gospel in the malls and on the lawns of hundreds of university campuses throughout this land. They have been mocked, rocked, stoned, mobbed, beaten, jailed, cursed and ridiculed by the students. Yet this former university professor and his wife have seen the miracle-working power of God transform thousands of lives on university campuses.